by Tony Krupa, Terry Snow, Harvey McLeod

Water Motions, Inc.
Winter Park, Florida

ACKNOWLEDGEMENTS

The publishing of SKI TIPS required the help of many people. We greatly appreciate the patience and backing of Walt Meloon, Jr. and Correct Craft, Inc., the diligent and creative photography of Barbara Young, the skiing and photography of champion water skier Rick McCormick, the hours of typing by Tamyra Krupa and the creative ideas of Gary Krupa.

We would also like to thank the American Water Ski Association, Spray Publications, Inc., Watersports, Inc., The Ski Rack, The Central Florida Water Ski Club, Tony Bates, Bob Braun, Don Bucher, Jim Corley, Shirley Duke, Ceel Pasternak, Hugh Petersen, Barbara Peterson, John Shoemaker and Russ Stiffler.

And our special thanks to Tony and Bonnie, Francis and Blanche, and Harvey and Pauline.

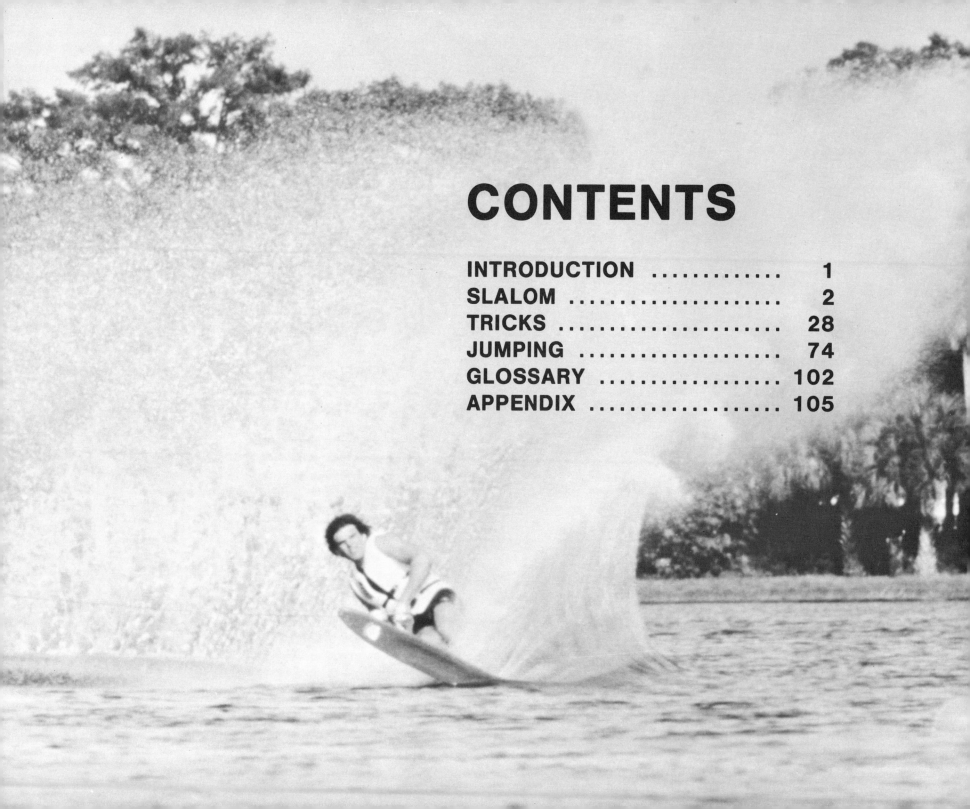

CONTENTS

INTRODUCTION

SKI TIPS is written for all water skiers and water ski enthusiasts. It teaches beginning skiers the fundamentals of proper skiing and introduces them to slalom course skiing, trick skiing and jumping. It offers competitive skiers an up to date guide on the newest practice techniques, tricks and equipment. And it gives coaches, parents and observers a basis for instructing and helping aspiring skiers.

The publication of SKI TIPS reflects the surge in interest in water skiing. In just over a 50 year history, nearly 20 million people annually participate in water skiing. This growth can be traced to three sources. First, the increasing interest in participation sports, in particular boating, has exposed more people to water skiing. Second, the big improvements made in water skiing equipment, such as better boats and high performance skis, have made learning to ski easy. Third, and probably most significant, the emergence of a group of water skiing superstars has helped bring competitive water skiing to the public through TV, newspapers and magazines.

These factors have made competitive water skiing a major sporting event. Such stars as Wayne Grimditch, Rick McCormick, Robert Kempton, Mike Hazelwood and Liz Allan Shetter have traveled all over the world competing in amateur and professional tournaments.

Wherever they go they have generated new excitement and interest in the sport. And like in other major sports, they have their own group of followers cheering them on.

But even with world and national attention focused on the superstars of water skiing, it has been at the recreational and local competitive level where water skiing has had its greatest growth. Today many recreational skiers diligently ski every day and future stars compete with skiers of comparable ability at amateur tournaments across the country. These skiers vary in age, occupations, background, and skiing skills, but they all have one thing in common, a desire to improve their water skiing.

All these skiers, recreational, amateur and professional will benefit from the up to date and complete instruction offered in SKI TIPS. Each chapter is exclusively devoted to explaining and illustrating one of the three competitive water skiing events; slalom, tricks and jumping. Each event is taught from the beginning stages and gone through to the most advanced skiing techniques. The information offered represents years of skiing experience and success, and when used properly will quicken a skier's progress and understanding of water skiing.

SLALOM

Slalom skiing is the most popular form of water skiing, attracting nearly 90% of all those who participate in the sport. It offers physically rewarding exercise and is generally the first major progression a beginning skier makes.

Not surprising is the fact that slalom skiing is also the most participated in of the competitive water ski events. But perhaps surprising is that a top competitive slalom course skier can accelerate a ski from 36 mph to 70 mph in less than 150 feet, turn a ski at almost 90 degree angles and throw a wall of spray over 20 feet in the air.

The competitive slalom skier uses strength, coordination and practice to successfully negotiate a slalom course. The slalom course used consists of six evenly spaced turn buoys, three on each side a row of eight boat gates (see diagram). The skier skis through the entrance gates, around the outside of each turn buoy and finishes through the exit gates while the boat maintains a straight path and constant speed.

In competition the starting speed is optional to the skier but usually falls between 26 mph and 36 mph depending on the skier's age and sex. If the skier successfully makes all the buoys at the starting speed, the speed is increased two mph for the next pass. If this pass is completed the speed is increased again by two mph. This procedure continues until the skier misses a buoy, falls or completes a perfect pass at the maximum boat speed for his or her division, 34 or 36 mph (see appendix).

A skier who successfully negotiates a pass at the maximum division boat speed continues skiing. Only now instead of increasing the boat speed after each successful pass, the standard 75 foot ski rope is shortened. This procedure starts by first taking 15 feet off the tow rope. If this pass is made, the procedure continues, shortening the rope in predetermined lengths until the skier misses or falls. The skier who scores the most consecutive buoys from the division starting speed wins.

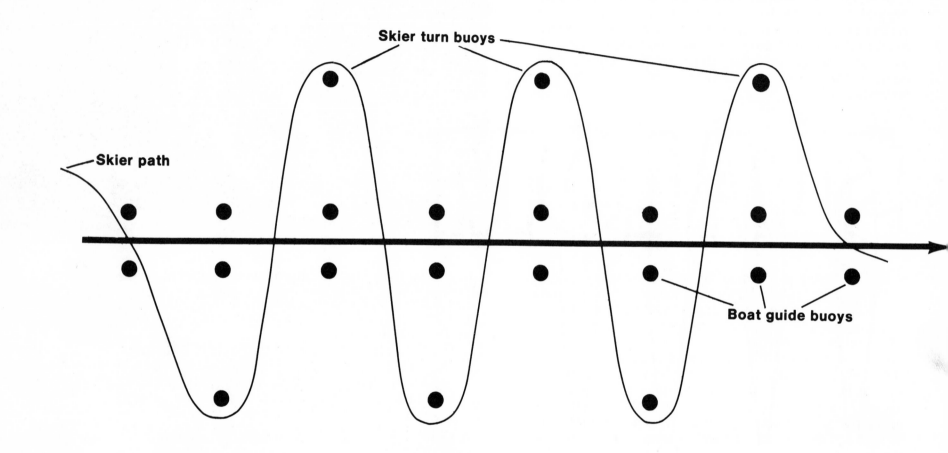

Skier turn buoys

Skier path

Boat guide buoys

SLALOM COURSE

(Not to Scale)

SLALOM SKIS AND EQUIPMENT

Selecting the proper slalom ski requires personal evaluation. Unlike trick and jump skis there is no slalom ski design that fits everyone's needs. All skiers must find a ski that conforms with their skiing style. A ski must feel comfortable, perform consistently and compliment a skier's ability and physical characteristics.

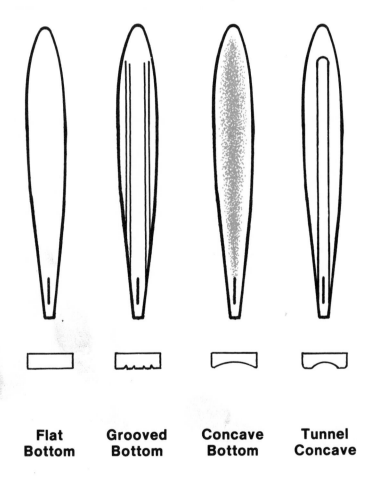

Flat Bottom **Grooved Bottom** **Concave Bottom** **Tunnel Concave**

Ski Bottom Design

There are four types of slalom skis to choose from: flat bottom, grooved bottom, concave and tunnel concave *(see illustration)*.

1. The flat bottom ski is used primarily by beginners. This design makes a ski stable at slower speeds and makes learning and deep water starts easier.
2. The grooved bottom is used primarily by recreational and intermediate skiers. It is designed for better tracking and holding power than the flat bottom ski.
3. The concave bottom is used by intermediate and competitive skiers. The concave helps prevent the ski from slipping during a turn.
4. The tunnel concave is an exaggerated concave ski that is used by intermediate and competitive skiers. The deeper and narrower concave gives the ski exceptional holding power for high speed turning and cutting.

Ski Size

Choosing the proper slalom ski size is very important to enhance skier performance. It is largely a function of the skier's weight and boat speed as shown in the following slalom ski size chart. But before relying exclusively on the chart, consider these other factors when selecting a ski size.

1. Beginning skiers need ski stability. The extra surface area of larger skis adds more control at slower speeds and reduces the drag on deep water starts.
2. Outboards and inboard/outboards generally are slower accelerating than inboards. A larger ski makes take offs easier behind a slow accelerating boat.
3. Heavy skiers skiing at slow speeds will have more control and use less effort with a larger ski.
4. Skiers near a weight borderline should probably go to the larger ski size.

Slalom Ski Size Chart

Skier Weight	Boat Speed	Ski Length
80 lbs and under	18-30 mph	60-62"
81 to 125 lbs	24-36 mph	63-64"
126 to 180 lbs	24-36 mph	65-66"
Over 180 lbs	26-36 mph	67-70"

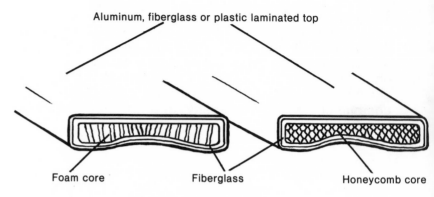

Aluminum, fiberglass or plastic laminated top

Foam core   Fiberglass   Honeycomb core

Ski Cross Section

Ski Construction

Wood. Wood skis are a good choice for the beginning skier since there are a wide variety of inexpensive styles available from the basic flat bottom to the competitive concave models. Before buying a wood ski, check for the quality of the laminations and make sure the ski has either a hard waterproof varnish or epoxy finish.

Fiberglass/foam. The fiberglass/foam skis are recommended for the beginning, recreational and intermediate skier. They usually have the advantage of lower maintenance than wood skis but normally do not possess the strength, durability or acceleration of the higher priced honeycomb or carbon graphite skis.

Fiberglass/aluminum honeycomb and carbon graphite. The honeycomb and carbon graphite skis are generally used by competitive skiers, but are excellent investments for the intermediate or serious recreation skier who wants a durable, top performance ski. Both skis are made to withstand a great deal of stress and most have different flexes over the length of the ski for very quick turning and exceptional acceleration capabilities.

Performance Characteristics

As your skiing ability progresses, ski design becomes more critical. Demands are placed on a ski to perform with your style. You become interested in the capacity of the ski to turn, accelerate and decelerate. These characteristics are associated with ski length, width, bottom design, flex and edges.

1. **Length.** Long skis are more stable, less sensitive to body movement and accelerate faster than shorter skis. Short skis generally turn quicker and decelerate faster.
2. **Width.** Wide skis accelerate faster than narrower skis but do not decelerate as quickly. Extra width also contributes to stability.
3. **Bottom design.** The concave and tunnel concave skis are stable turning skis at fast boat speeds. Flatness in the bottom tail of a concave or tunnel concave ski usually increases acceleration.
4. **Ski flex.** Stiff skis accelerate faster than more flexible skis but generally do not turn as quickly.
5. **Edges.** A beveled edge makes turning easier. The bottom edge of the bevel controls more of the turning capabilities while the top edge of the bevel controls more of the acceleration and deceleration of the ski. Generally, sharp edges increase acceleration and round edges make turning easier, but with slower acceleration.

There are many performance characteristic tradeoffs in slalom ski selection. To decide what kind of ski you need, analyze your skiing ability and match it to the performance characteristics of the ski. For instance, if you use a slalom course and have trouble reaching the buoys you might need a faster accelerating ski. A larger ski or a flat tail bottom design could help. On the other hand, if you have difficulty slowing down before a turn you may need a smaller or more flexible ski. Or if you do a lot of rough water skiing and your ski bounces and is uncontrollable in the turns, you may need a stiffer or longer ski.

A final point to consider when selecting a slalom ski is that finding a ski with the performance characteristics you want still might not satisfy all your skiing needs. The most important ski characteristic is a steady and consistent feel. A good ski is one you feel comfortable on and confident using.

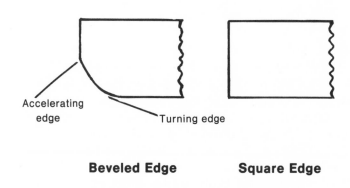

Beveled Edge   **Square Edge**

Bindings

The front slalom binding must fit snugly to maintain proper control of the ski. Reinforcement straps over the instep of the foot and around the heel help support the foot and add to a more secure fit. The binding material should be either a soft rubber or a nylon reinforced rubber that has good resilience and stretches to fit the shape of the foot; if possible avoid plastics and brittle rubber.

The purpose of the rear binding is to hold the rear foot firmly on top of the ski. It should be mounted so the rear foot touches or almost touches the front heel. Some skiers use a rear heel binding for added secureness while others prefer to use only a toe binding. Using the rear heel piece or only the toe binding is a personal choice. The important points are to have the rear foot comfortable, secure and close to the front foot.

The binding rubber is usually fastened directly to the ski with either metal or plastic brackets. Before using your ski be sure the bindings are trimmed so that no rubber hangs over the edge of the ski. Protrusions can catch water and cause falls.

Flotation

The use of a slalom jacket is mandatory for all sanctioned slalom ski events and is necessary for anyone who skis. The slalom vest, whether ensolite or nylon, offers flotation and rib protection that a ski belt and wet suit cannot. To be beneficial, a vest must fit snugly around the chest and allow for unrestricted arm movement. Too small a jacket is too restrictive for moving and breathing and too large a jacket slips and provides very little flotation or rib protection. Pick a vest with large arm openings and a slit up the middle of the back.

Ropes and Handles

The official slalom rope is 75 feet long and made of ¼" braided polypropylene. Other types of rope that do not stretch or break can be used but are only second best. The majority of the manufacturers produce the rope in two pieces: a 70 foot rope and a five foot handle attachment. The slalom rope is also available with pre-measured shortening loops for the slalom course skier.

The best rope handles are made of rubber coated metal. They offer maximum durability and easy grip.

Periodically check the rope and handle attachment for wear, frayed loops and knots which shorten and weaken the rope. Then make the necessary repairs before you ski.

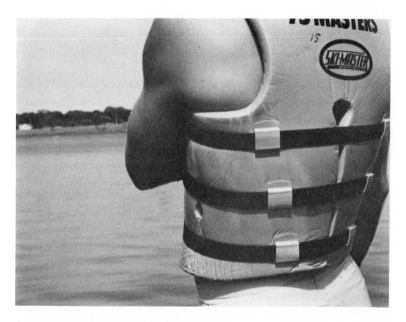

Large arm openings and a slit up the back allow for maximum freedom of movement and for the jacket to mold to your body.

Gloves

Slalom gloves are an intregal part of a skier's equipment. They help give a better grip on the handle and also improve the skier's pull. Gloves are also excellent protection against callous build up. The extra padding and skin coverage helps prevent chafing and rope burns.

LEARNING TO SLALOM

You are ready to learn to slalom after you have attained the ability to consistently cross the wakes on two skis. In most cases this requires very little time. Many people are capable of slalom skiing the same day they learn to ski.

Your first slalom skiing decision is picking the foot you want to ski forward with. Determining which foot to use generally does not require much effort; it should be natural. If you do have difficulty deciding, ski on two skis and lift one ski out of the water and then put it back down and lift the other. Pick the stance that feels the most comfortable and gives you the most balance.

Dropping a Ski

To drop a ski, begin skiing on two skis at about 20 to 24 mph, or about 15 to 18 mph if you are a child or light weight skier. With your head up, your back straight and your knees and arms slightly bent, lift your drop ski slightly off the water. Be sure to hold the tip of the ski above water so it doesn't catch and cause a fall. After lifting the ski a few times, loosen the heel of the ski you are dropping so you can pull your foot free from the binding. Now instead of lifting the ski, pull your foot out of the binding. Maintain your balance by dragging your toes in the water behind your forward foot. Let your foot drag until you feel steady. Then set your foot on the back of the ski and slowly ease it toward the binding. When you feel your toes entering the binding give your foot a careful push the rest of the way into the binding.

Shirely Duke demonstrates dropping a ski. Notice her body position, head up, back straight, etc., and how her weight is placed on the slalom ski, released off the drop ski, before her foot is pulled free of the binding.

Deep Water Start

The deep water start can be accomplished in two different ways. One method is to start with both feet in the bindings, the other is to trail the rear foot until your ski is on top of the water. The one foot method is usually more effective for heavier skiers while women and lighter skiers generally prefer to have both feet in the bindings.

The following information assumes the skier is right foot forward. If you are left foot forward the technique remains the same; simply substitute left for right and right for left.

To start with both feet in the bindings, keep your knees bent, sit on top of the ski and place the rope on the left side of the ski. As the boat takes off lean slightly away from the rope, a right foot forward skier leans to the right. When the ski breaks water begin standing up, but maintain a slight cut until your ski is on top of the water.

To start with your rear foot free, bend your front leg so your knee is pressed close to your chest and place the rope on the left side of the ski. As the boat takes off angle the ski away from the rope in a slight cut and use the trailing foot as a rudder for control and balance. Hold this position until the ski is on top of the water, then straighten up. When you have gained your balance slowly slide your back foot into the binding.

Deep Water Start

(Illustrated for a right foot forward skier)

SLALOM FUNDAMENTALS

Development of the proper skiing position is necessary for the beginning skier to gain control of his or her ski. There are four basic points to adhere to.

1. Your back must be straight or slightly arched backward.
2. Your knees must be slightly bent to absorb the shock of waves and wakes.
3. Your arms must be slightly bent to act as shock cords between your body and the boat.
4. Your weight must be evenly distributed on both feet.

Crossing the Wakes

When you cross the wakes establish the proper skiing position: back straight, arms and knees slightly bent and your weight evenly distributed on the ski. Then put the ski into an angled cut, lower your shoulder that is farthest from the boat and lean away from the pull of the boat. This technique makes the ski knife through, not bounce off, the wakes.

Quite often the beginning slalom skier is apprehensive when crossing the wakes. Many times the skier makes a turn, cuts for the wake and then stops the cut before crossing over the wakes. This flattens the ski allowing more ski surface area to hit the wake, resulting in the ski flying or bouncing off the water. It is this timidness that ususally causes falls. Approach the wakes with care, but learn to ski through them aggressively.

Ski across the wakes with an angled cut and your pulling shoulder lowered.

Turning

Establishing the proper cross grip on a vertically held handle is necessary to maximize the strength of a turn. Generally, if you are a left foot forward skier you should place your left hand on top of the handle and if you are right foot forward you should place your right hand on top. After choosing the proper grip you are ready to learn how to turn.

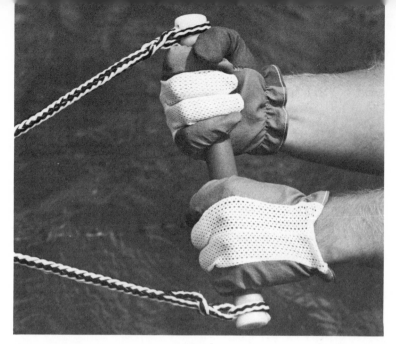

The cross grip, also called baseball grip, is used to maximize the strength of a turn and the pull out of the turn.

There are three parts in the complete turn: the preturn reach, the turn and the pull out of the turn.

1. **The preturn reach.** The preturn reach is necessary to slow the ski and prepare for the turn. As you approach a turn, hold the handle vertically with the proper cross grip then release your outside hand from the handle and extend the handle straight out from your side.

2. **The turn.** There are three simultaneous movements in the turn: pulling the rope in towards your chest, turning your head and shoulders into the turn and arching your back.

3. **The pull.** The pull is held from the turn through both wakes to generate the speed necessary to reach a position on the other side of the wakes to set up for the next turn. It is accomplished by having both of your hands on the handle at the end of the turn, your back straight or arched back, the handle down at your hips and your shoulder farthest from the boat; the pulling shoulder lowered.

The preturn reach slows the ski and places the skier in the proper position for making the turn.

Common Turning Mistakes and Remedies

1. Leaning back while initiating the turn brings the turning section of the ski out of the water and stops the turn. Keep your weight evenly distributed on the ski.

2. Pulling the rope over your head to absorb slack line prevents you from getting a solid pull from the turn and places you in an incorrect turning position. Slack line can be eliminated by slowing the ski. Establish the preturn reach and pull the handle toward your chest when turning.

3. Using two hands while turning is cumbersome and restrictive. To start the turn, always let go with your outside hand to get into the preturn reach and then grab the handle with the released hand during the turn.

4. Holding the handle with the wrong hand during the preturn reach restricts the turn. When you are on the right side of the boat use your left hand for the preturn reach. Likewise, on the left side use your right hand.

Pulling the handle over your head places you in an incorrect turning position.

Reaching forward causes you to bend at the waist and can result in a bad turn or fall.

5. Reaching forward causes you to bend forward at the waist and can result in falls over the front of the ski. Reach straight out from your side with your back straight.

6. Looking at the boat while making a turn prevents the ski from turning sharply. (The ski tends to follow where you look.) Turn your head and shoulders into the turn.

7. Bending forward at the waist after the turn causes you to get pulled forward while crossing the wakes. Keep your back straight or arched backward and the handle down at your hips when you cross the wakes.

8. Letting the handle get away from your body before getting to the wakes pulls you out of the proper skiing position, stops acceleration and can result in a fall. Keep the handle in close to your body from the turn through the wakes.

SKIING THE SLALOM COURSE

The boat speed for your initial try through the slalom course depends on your weight and skiing ability. It can range from 15 mph for small children to about 30 mph for heavier or more experienced skiers. Pick a speed where you have control of your ski and the ability to make buoys. For the majority of skiers this speed will be between 22 and 26 mph.

Your objective on the first runs through the course is to establish the ability to ski around the six turn buoys. This is accomplished by using the three turn characteristics: the preturn reach, the turn and the pull; on each buoy turn.

Begin slalom course skiing by eliminating the use of the entrance and exit gates on the first few attempts through the course (see diagram). Ski wide to the outside of the first right side turn buoy and establish the preturn reach with your inside arm. Start your turn before you reach the buoy so you are in your pull as you pass it. Ski as close to the down course side of the buoy as possible and maintain your angle of cut through both wakes. This allows you to reach the other side of the course with enough time to slow the ski for the next turn.

When approaching the remaining buoys, make a gradual change from the outside pulling edge of your ski to the inside turning edge. Again establish the preturn reach, ski wide of the buoy and initiate your turn so you are heading back into the course before passing the buoy (see diagram).

The beginning slalom course skier should eliminate the use of the entrance and exit gates. The objective is to ski around the six turn buoys to gain a feel for the rhythm of the course.

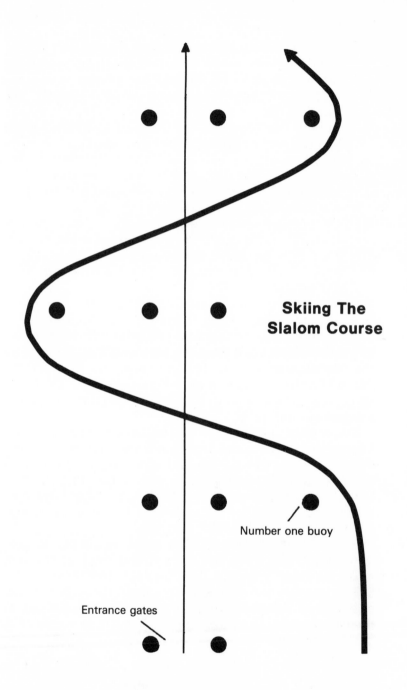

Skiing The Slalom Course

Number one buoy

Entrance gates

Learning how hard to go through the gate to make a good first buoy turn requires practice. Your perception of how to do it depends to a great extent on your skiing style. An aggressive, quick turning skier can come through the gates fast and make a quick first buoy turn while a rhythm skier should come through the gates slower and make a long sweeping turn. Each method is correct, when it works. Experiment with your gate approaches and find a technique that is comfortable. When you have found the best technique stay with it and concentrate on gate and first buoy consistency.

Entrance Gates

Once you are consistently making all six buoys, begin including the entrance and exit gates. To include the entrance gates, cut approximately 50 feet outside the left boat wake before entering the course. Then line up on the left side row of turn buoys and the position of the boat in the gates.

Begin your cut through the entrance gates with the handle in at your waist and your right shoulder slightly down. Aim the cut so you ski close to the right gate buoy. This technique adds a foot or two to your distance from the gates to the first buoy. The extra distance becomes more important at faster speeds and shorter rope lengths *(see diagram)*.

Going through the entrance gates is similar to getting a good pull from one buoy to the next, as the pull must be held from the turn through the wakes. The difference is your ski must now pass through the two gate buoys. Avoid either pulling harder or easing up at the last moment to make the gate. Time it so your pull is hardest through the gates.

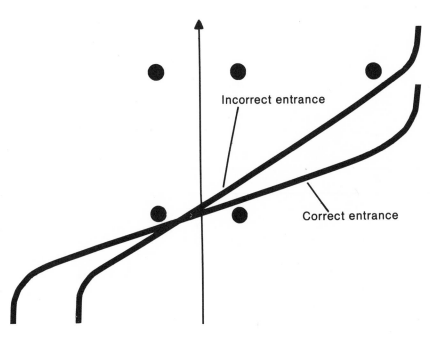

Gate Entrance Diagram

Number One Buoy

Every slalom course skier stresses the importance of getting a good turn on the first buoy. What is desired is an early turn with a good pull to set up for the second buoy and to establish a smooth pace for the rest of the course.

To get an early turn you must get wide of the first buoy before making the turn *(see diagram).* Being wide allows you to initiate the turn sooner and be in your pull, heading back into the course as you pass the buoy. Getting wide necessitates having more speed and a harder pull when going through the gates. The more speed, the quicker you arrive at the desired width.

The amount of speed you must attain to get wide will largely depend on the boat speed and the rope length you are skiing at. At slower speeds and longer rope lengths you will have more time to negotiate the turn and do not have to generate as much speed. However, as the rope length is shortened and the boat speed is increased you have less time to reach the buoy and you will need to acquire more speed to reach the desired wide position.

Along with the increase in speed comes the requirement of changing edges and slowing the ski before the turn. Learning how quickly to change edges and when to establish the preturn reach requires practice. If you are a left foot forward skier you will be making a good side turn on buoy one and will be able to have a fast gate and be able to make a quick turn. On the other hand, if you are right foot forward you will be making a weak side turn and generally must come into the buoy at a slower speed to be able to slow the ski before the turn.

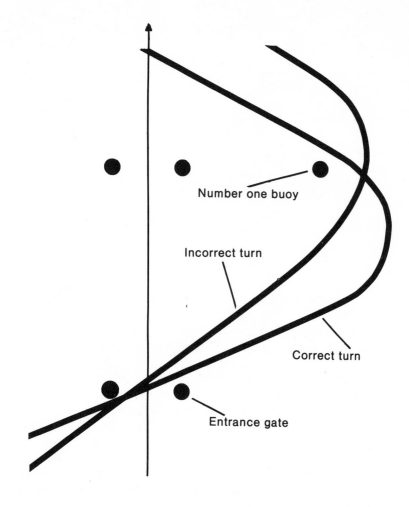

Number One Buoy Approach and Turn

As you approach the first buoy
quickly establish the preturn reach
and begin the turn into the
course before passing the buoy.

Weak Side Turn

Most skiers have good and bad turning sides that become obvious as they ski through the course. A left foot forward skier generally has less control turning to the right and a right foot forward skier has less control turning to the left.

There are three characteristics in a bad turning side: difficulty in getting the ski on edge to slow the ski, a tendency to reach in front of the body instead of to the side and difficulty in keeping a good angle of cut while crossing the wakes.

Because your body is in a different position on your weak side turn, you should do different things to get the proper turn and pull.

1. Bend your knees more as you are coming into the turn. This slows the ski by placing more weight on the front of the ski.
2. Lift your pulling arm slightly higher before the turn. This helps keep your back straight since you have to be in an upright stance to reach high. It also helps keep your weight evenly distributed on the ski.
3. Exaggerate your head and shoulder turn during the ski turn. This extra effort quickens the turn and establishes a good angle of cut out of the turn.

Acceleration and Deceleration

Proper acceleration is especially important when you ski through a slalom course. Accelerating from the turn through the wakes gets you to the other side of the course with enough time to properly set up for the next buoy turn.

Acceleration develops from the start of the turn and is a product of angle of cut, force of pull and length of pull. Increasing the angle of cut draws the shortest line to the other side of the course and increases ski acceleration since the boat is moving at a constant speed.

Acceleration is a function of body position. Keep your back straight, push with your legs, hold the handle close to your hip and lower your pulling shoulder.

The force of the pull is usually associated with strength, but it is more a function of body positioning. You can maximize your pull and increase acceleration by keeping your back arched backward, pushing with your legs, keeping the handle close to your hip from the end of the turn through both wakes and by lowering your pulling shoulder.

Every time you accelerate in a slalom course you will have to decelerate, slow the ski, before initiating another turn. Deceleration is achieved by establishing the proper preturn reach and stretching your upper body in toward the wakes. This technique places the ski on the inside edge, reduces the ski surface area on the water and allows the ski to sit deeper in the water, causing drag and thus slowing the ski.

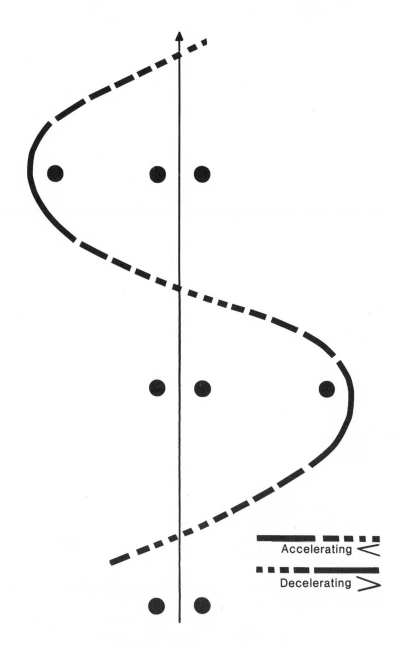

Acceleration/Deceleration

— — — — Accelerating

· · · · · Decelerating

Photo Spray Publications, Inc.

The ski must be placed on edge to decelerate for the turn.

Slalom Course Progression

Improving your slalom course skiing is actually developing the basic fundamentals already described. If you are falling around a particular buoy or having difficulty making the entire course, look for possible errors in your gate approach, first buoy turn, weak side turns and acceleration and deceleration.

Once you are successfully making the entire course you should begin increasing your boat speed in two mph increments. Each time you make a higher speed, increase your boat speed, until you are making the entire course at the maximum speed for your division. At this point keep the boat speed constant and shorten the rope length by the predetermined lengths.

Photo Don Bucher

SHORT LINE SLALOM

The fundamentals become more important and obvious as you advance to short line slalom. As the rope is shortened you have less time to turn because you are generating faster speeds. Your path begins to resemble a zig-zag, losing its smooth symmetry. Turns are made quicker, pulls harder and deceleration faster.

There are two plateaus of learning reached by this caliber of skier. The first occurs at an 18.25 meter rope length (15 off), the first line shortening. The second plateau occurs at the fourth line shortening, a 13 meter rope (32 off), a level where you are faced with the goals of perfecting your timing and forcing the ski to turn.

18.25 Meters (15 off)

The difference between skiing long line and 18.25 meters begins with the approach through the gates *(see diagram)*. A sharper angle is needed with the shorter rope length to generate the necessary speed to get into the proper wide position for the first buoy turn.

The shorter line also increases acceleration during the pull and necessitates decelerating quicker for the first buoy turn. The quick establishment of the preturn reach is necessary for achieving this deceleration and making an early turn.

The pull out of the turn resembles that of long line, only with more emphasis on holding the angle of cut. This means quickly turning your head and shoulders into the turn, lowering your pulling shoulder from the turn through the wakes and quickly arching your back after the turn. These three maneuvers put you into a controlled stance and maximize your acceleration.

The quicker turn at the shorter line lengths is sometimes accompanied by slack rope. The slack results from the sharp turn but developes primarily from not adequately slowing the ski before initiating the turn. To eliminate slack, ski wide of the buoy and quickly establish the proper preturn reach.

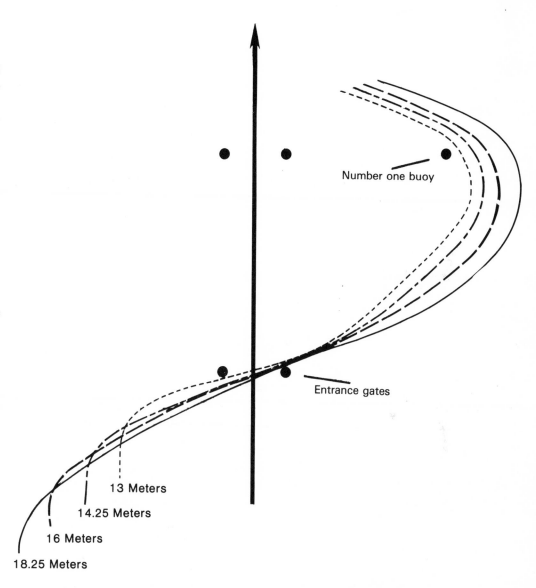

Number one buoy

Entrance gates

13 Meters

14.25 Meters

16 Meters

18.25 Meters

Gate Approach for Short Line Slalom

16 and 14.25 Meters (22 and 28 Off)

The second and third line shortenings are skied similar to the first with the following exceptions. First, your angle of approach through the gates must be increased to reach the buoys with the shorter rope. Secondly, you are generating more speed and have to change edges harder and establish the preturn reach quicker to decelerate. Finally, there is more of a tendency to get pulled forward while crossing the wakes. Concentrate on keeping your weight evenly distributed as you begin your pull and hold the pull through both wakes.

13 Meters (32 Off)

Skiing 13 meters is a transition for most good slalom skiers, because anyone who can get to it has the fundamentals and technique to make it. What makes 13 meters different is that you must force your body to do things much quicker and harder. You must force yourself to establish the preturn reach and to hold the angle of cut at very fast speeds.

Getting wide for the first buoy at 13 meters requires an extreme angle through the gates, almost touching both gate buoys with the ski. To reach the first buoy and make a good turn, your gate timing must be perfected so that each gate entry is the same. Always line up on the left side row of turn buoys and the boat position in the gates for a gate entry reference point.

Decelerating for the first buoy has to be done quickly to compensate for the additional speed generated from the increased angle of cut through the gates. Force the ski on edge with your legs and get your reaching arm fully extended from your side shortly after you cross the second wake. There is little time for making corrections and poor turns are often the result of having too much speed coming into the buoy and not getting into the preturn reach quickly.

The turn, angle of cut and pull are very critical at this line length. Concentrate on turning the ski sharply by forcing the handle towards your chest. Immediately lower your pulling shoulder and pull with it from the turn through both wakes. This will keep the sharp angle of cut that is necessary to reach the next buoy.

12 Meters (35 Off) and Beyond

A skier who can successfully run a perfect pass on a 13 meter rope has developed the skills and knowledge for running shorter line lengths. The fundamentals remain the same, except they are exaggerated. The keys are proper acceleration, deceleration and luck.

SLALOM COURSE PRACTICE

Learning how to practice your slalom course skiing is as important as knowing the proper skiing techniques. The most critical practice decisions you will be making are deciding at what speeds to ski, when to raise the boat speed, by how much to increase that speed and how to analyze your skiing mistakes.

Perhaps the most important point to remember when you are trying to decide at what speeds to ski, is that you must spend considerable practice time going through the course at speeds where you can make all the buoys. By making buoys you are learning how to turn your ski, gaining confidence in your slalom course skiing, establishing consistency and learning the rhythm of slalom course skiing.

Begin each practice session at a speed of four to six mph less than what you are capable of making. For instance, if 30 mph is the maximum speed you can make through the course, then start your practice sessions at either 24 or 26 mph. After successfully completing a slower speed pass, raise the boat speed two mph. When you reach a speed where you can not make all the buoys, spend three or four passes trying to make it. If you still are unable to make the buoys, lower the boat speed about one mph and try to slowly ease into the faster speed. If after a few sessions no progress is made try this method: Increase the speed two mph over your maximum. Take a few passes at this faster speed and then slow down to the speed you are trying to make. Sometimes this faster speed helps prepare you for reacting quicker for the speed you are having difficulty with.

Practicing short line slalom is similar to practicing long line. You should always start your practice session at a speed and rope length that enables you to make all the buoys on the first three passes. However, in short line skiing more emphasis is placed on learning how to react to the shorter rope length than to having the required boat speed. If you can't make the buoys at the shorter rope lengths, have the boat speed lowered one or two mph until you can. Then when you are able to make all the buoys slowly increase the boat speed until you are going the required speed.

Mix your practice session by skiing half of it at speeds and rope lengths you can make and the other half at the faster speed or shorter rope lengths you are trying to make. Doing this allows you to learn how to turn at speeds you can control and pushes your progress by making you try speeds and rope lengths that are difficult for you.

An average slalom workout consist of six to eight passes. Determining how many slalom passes you should take largely depends on your strength and ability. Consider these factors:

1. Beginners should ski the slalom course as often as they can.
2. Children and light weight skiers generally have more endurance than large adults.
3. If you ski more than one session a day, a fewer number of passes per session might be adequate.
4. If you ski other events, energy preservation might necessitate lighter workouts.
5. Conditioning might require taking more passes.

Analyze your slalom course skiing by looking at the turning characteristics described earlier. If you are having difficulty making progress be sure you are using the basics. Also look through the list of common turning mistakes. Especially take a careful look to be sure you are not leaning back while turning, not letting the handle get away from your body before crossing the wakes and not reaching forward.

COMPETITIVE SLALOM SKIING

One of the main concerns of a slalom skier entering a tournament is to be physically prepared. Many competitors prefer to taper their practice sessions a day or two before competing. This allows their muscles to relax and to gain strength for the tournament. The amount of tapering or the amount of practice you do before a tournament depends on your physical characteristics and the amount of energy you have.

When you arrive at the ski site familiarize yourself with the slalom course and the surroundings. Note any unusual obstacles near the course; i.e., boat docks, shoreline walls, jumps, etc. While other divisions are skiing watch how the boat path is driven and how the skiers negotiate the entrance and exit gates. Analyze these factors so you are totally prepared when your ski turn arrives.

Your goals the first pass through the course are to gain a feel for the course, the driver, the conditions and loosen up your tightness and nervousness. Pick a starting speed that you are capable of making under any conditions.

After the first pass you should start skiing more like your practices; relaxed and aggressive. However, mistakes can be made. In competition these mistakes can become magnified and the natural reaction to correct them takes place at one buoy. Learn to ski one buoy at a time and learn to ski with your mistakes by slightly compensating for them on each of the remaining buoys. Remember, no slalom course is made on one buoy, it takes all six to get credit for the pass.

Analyze your slalom mistakes by looking at the basic turn characteristics.

Photo Rick McCormick

World Slalom Champion Bob LaPoint

ADVERSE WATER CONDITIONS

Finding ski sites which offer protection from all wind directions and waves is rare. Therefore slalom skiers will ski under unfavorable water conditions from time to time. Performances are generally down under these circumstances but with practice good scores can be achieved.

Wind is the biggest culprit of rough water. Three types of wind conditions can be expected: cross wind, head wind and tail wind. The three types should be handled in slightly different ways with some overriding similarities. When skiing in any uncertain water conditions, bend your knees more, but most importantly have confidence and relax.

When skiing in side winds change your rhythm from one side of the course to the other. When skiing into the wind the pull must be held longer to get wide for the next buoy. With the wind at your back, the pull should be short and hard. This gets you across the course earlier with more time to decelerate and prepare for the next turn.

A head wind is the easiest condition to ski under since the wind helps slow you down. Your main concern now is to hold your pull longer than normal to reach the proper width for the next buoy turn. Your weight should be farther back on the ski when decelerating and making turns to prevent the ski from slowing too quickly and to prevent the front of the ski from diving during the turn.

Skiing the course with a tail wind is similar to skiing at a speed one to two miles faster than normal. Deceleration becomes critical. To compensate for this speed, make short, hard pulls to acquire all your acceleration by the second wake. This gives you more time to change edges, establish the preturn reach and prepare for the next buoy turn. If conditions are extreme and decelerating is difficult, bend your knees forward before the turn to place more weight on the front of the ski.

Back wash, waves and rollers, which bounce off neighboring boats and shoreline walls, have always plagued slalom skiers. The best way of approaching this situation is to relax and ski like normal. Maintain your aggressiveness and concentrate on keeping proper form with your knees slightly bent.

Knowing how to ski in adverse water conditions is only a small part of successful skiing when the water is not perfect. There is no substitute for the experience, control and comfort practice gives.

Learning to ski in bad water should be a reaction. To learn how to react you must practice when the wind is blowing and when conditions aren't ideal. Don't neglect the opportunity to practice in adverse conditions. It is the only means of learning how to ski in them.

Photo Rick McCormick

SLALOM COURSE DRIVING

To become a good slalom driver you must be familiar with the driving pattern and technique necessary to drive through a slalom course. If you are an inexperience driver, you should drive through the course without the skier until this familiarity is established *(see diagram)*.

As a slalom driver you have three objectives: you must drive a straight line, hold a constant speed through the course and keep boat wakes through the course to a minimum.

Approach the course by aiming for the middle of the first set of gates while keeping the end of the course in sight. As the boat goes through the gates prepare for the skier's cut. When you feel the pull from the cut and the boat begins to move to the right, compensate by turning the wheel slightly to the left. When the skier cuts to the other side of the course from the first buoy, the boat is moved to the left and you must compensate again. Continue this technique at each buoy but be

very careful not to over compensate. The objective is to keep the boat in the center of the course.

The desired boat speed must be established before entering the course. As the skier begins cutting, the throttle must be advanced slightly and then backed down when the cut is eased. Your objective is to counteract the skier's pull and hold the same boat speed through the entire course. The key is anticipating the pulls and *gently* compensating for them.

A speedometer can be a good guide for finding the desired speed and for judging the amount of throttle necessary to compensate for the skier's pull. However, a speedometer has a tendency to fluctuate one or two mph while the actual speed may vary less. To be an effective driver, you must learn to *feel* the differences in speed and compensate for those differences by anticipation.

Your ability to hold a constant speed should be judged by using a stop watch to time the boat during each practice session. Getting times allows you to adjust for inaccuracies of the speedometer and also assures you that a skier gets pulled at his or her desired speed. *(See appendix for official times and tolerances.)*

A driver also has the responsibility of picking up a fallen skier. The first priority in picking up a skier is to check for the hand safety signal *(see appendix)*. If the signal has not been given, then return to the skier as quickly and safely as possible. If the skier has given the signal and appears to be all right, turn the boat around without causing waves that disrupt the practice area. To eliminate waves, slow the boat down and make as small a turning radius as possible and quickly get back into the boat path before picking up the skier. When the skier starts up again the boat should be driven in the ski course path or parallel to that path. Never aim the boat at an angle to the course or start wide outside the course since the boat wakes will eventually go through the ski area.

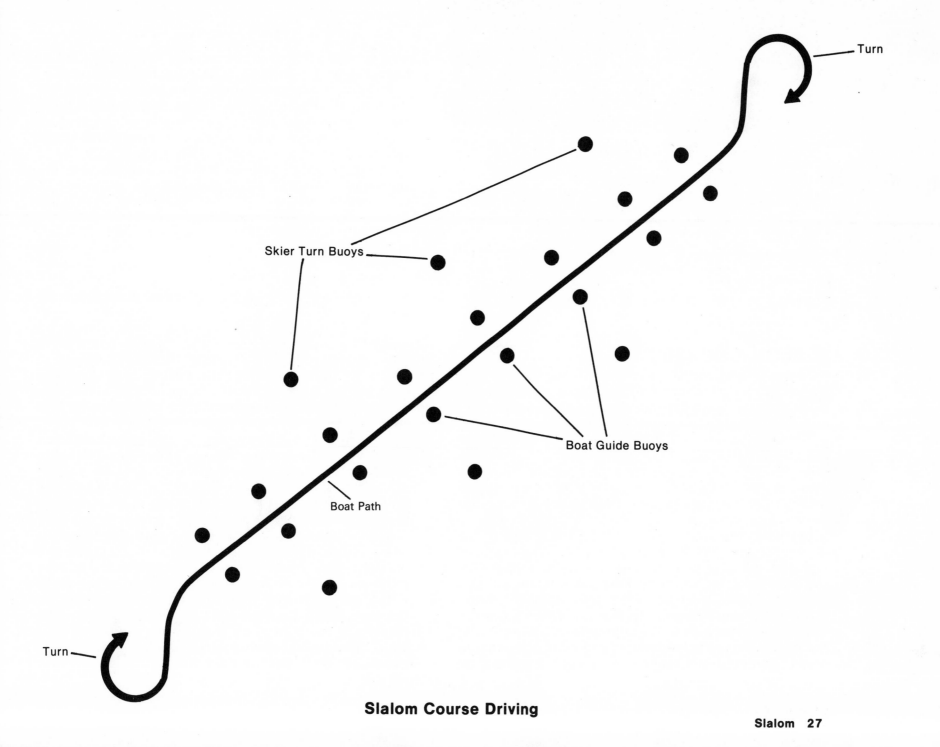

Turn

Skier Turn Buoys

Boat Guide Buoys

Boat Path

Turn

Slalom Course Driving

TRICKS

Trick skiing is *the* dynamic water ski event. All trick skiers have their own personalities that are expressed in their trick skiing. This individuality constantly helps develop changing trick styles, new tricks and better ways of doing old tricks.

Competitive trick skiing, perhaps more than any other event, reflects the fast development of water skiing. Recent innovations in techniques, practice, equipment and the surprisingly rapid development of Venezuelan and European skiers have pushed trick scores to new high levels. The present world record runs of over 7000 points consist of approximately 35 different tricks performed in 40 seconds of skiing: A remarkable accomplishment of speed, coordination and control.

The types of tricks done in competition are variations of turning 90, 180, 360, 540 and 720 degrees. They are divided into five categories.

1. Surface turns (tricks done on the surface of the water).
2. Wake turns (tricks that involve jumping off the boat wake and making turns in the air).
3. Stepover turns (tricks that involve lifting a ski or free foot over the tow rope while turning).
4. Toehold turns (tricks that require putting a foot in a toe strap on the bridle of the handle and then turning).
5. Combination turns (tricks that involve putting together wake turns with stepovers or wake turns with toeholds).

Competitive trick skiing is a demonstration of these various tricks within a time constraint. It usually consists of two 20-second intervals of skiing. Each interval is referred to as a "pass." In a pass the skier does as many tricks as he or she can perform. No trick can be repeated and there are no required tricks.

Each trick has a predetermined point value based on its difficulty. A skier receives the points for a trick if the judges (usually five) decide that the trick was done correctly. At the end of each pass all the trick points for the tricks done correctly are added together. If the skier falls during a pass, the skier's pass ends but the skier gets points for each trick done correctly to that point. The total points for both passes are then added together to arrive at a final score. The highest score wins.

The following is an example of a trick run performed by a relatively new competitor.

First Pass

Two Skis	Point Value	Judges Abbreviation
Side Slide 90	20	(SS)
Front to Back 180	30	(B)
Back to Front 180	30	(F)
Front to Front 360	40	(O)
Wake Front to Back 180	50	(WB)
Wake Back to Front 180	50	(WF)
Wake Front to Front 360	110	(WO)
First Pass Total Points	330	

Second Pass

One Ski		
Toe Front to Back 180	100	(TB)
Toe Back to Front 180	120	(TF)
Wake Toe Front to Back 180	150	(WTB)
Wake Toe Back to Front 180	180	(WTF)
Side Slide 90	70	(SS)
Front to Back 180	60	(B)
Back to Front 180	60	(F)
Second Pass Total	740	
Total Score	1070	

TRICK SKIS AND EQUIPMENT

Good trick skis have specific performance characteristics. These features, and not a high price tag, skier's name or brand name, make the skis perform.

Performance Characteristics

1. *Round top edges.* The top edge of the skis should be rounded off so water slides over the ski while turning.
2. *Large ski tip area.* The ski tip should have a substantial amount of ski area. It should not be severely tapered or pointed. Whether the tips are rounded or squared is of little skiing importance.
3. *Flat bottom.* The ski bottom should be flat, neither convex nor concave.
4. *Ski rocker.* The skis should have a gradual full length rocker or a small flat spot in the center with a gradual rocker over the remainder of the ski.
5. *Smooth bottom.* The bottom should be smooth, without grooves or small rudders.
6. *Light weight.* A trick ski should be light weight to turn easily and break from the wakes.

Construction

1. **_Wood._** Wood skis are usually less expensive than fiberglass skis and can make a good first investment if they have the performance characteristics already described. However, wood skis are generally susceptable to quick wearing and breaking from continual use.

2. **_Fiberglass/foam._** Fiberglass/foam skis are the least expensive fiberglass trick skis and are recommended for the beginner and intermediate skier. They tend to be more durable, lighter and offer better performance than wood skis.

3. **_Fiberglass/aluminum honeycomb._** Honeycomb trick skis offer the best performance and are used by competitors and serious recreational skiers. Their light weight and added buoyancy make them more maneuverable on the water and allow them to lift quickly and easily from the wake. Most honeycomb trick skis also have rubber edges that help reduce ski wear.

Ski Size

Minimum ski widths have been placed in the following ski size chart to reflect the trend towards wider skis. A potential trick ski buyer should check magazines, qualified sales personnel or ski manufacturer's data to make sure they are getting skis that reflect current ski knowledge and ski rules.

Skier Size	Ski Length	Minimum Ski Width
Junior (under 80 lbs.)	38"	8"
Up to 5'8" (160 lbs. max.)	40"	9 3/4"
5'9" to 6'2" (200 lbs. max.)	42"	9 3/4"
Over 6'2" (over 200 lbs.)	44"	9 3/4"

Generally, a skier with a weight or height near or on a borderline should go with the next trick ski size.

Bindings

Because trick skiers are constantly turning and jumping, they need to have perfect control of their skis. This control is enhanced by having bindings that fit snugly over the entire foot. A binding that allows the heel to move or the foot to slide is not good for trick skiing.

To achieve the proper fit, reinforcement straps must be placed around the heel and over the arch of the foot. The binding material should be flexible enough to mold around the foot, yet firm enough to offer support when performing tricks.

Trick skiing involves constantly trying new tricks and techniques. This can mean many falls, resulting in a substantial amount of binding use. With this in mind, trick bindings should be durable, perhaps even more so than in slalom or jumping. Use bindings made of flexible or nylon reinforced rubber. Avoid hard plastics and stiff rubber since they have a tendency to tear.

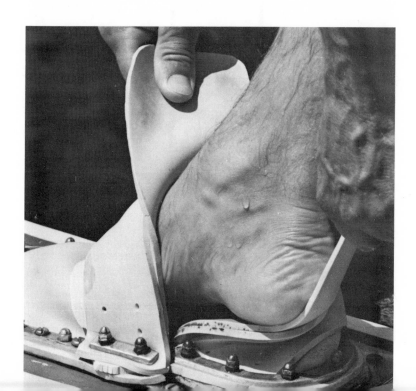

Binding Placement

The general rule for binding placement is to have the center of the instep ½" to 1" in front of the balance point of the ski. This point can be determined by laying the ski across your hand and finding the point where the ski balances.

The placement of the rear foot for one ski tricks is important for achieving one ski balance. How to place the rear toe piece depends on which foot is skied forward. The rear binding should be placed at a 45 degree angle with the inside of the rear ankle approximately two inches behind the heel of the front foot. Keeping the foot at this angle maximizes ski control and stability.

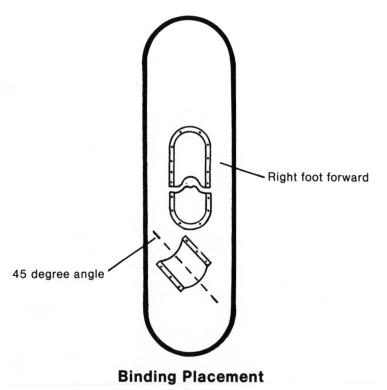

Binding Placement

Flotation

The beginning trick skier and the not so good swimmer should always wear a life vest. The life vest serves the dual purpose of flotation and body protection. It also takes the physical effort out of staying afloat after a fall. This helps preserve energy and allows for longer and more beneficial practice sessions.

You have probably noticed that most top trick competitors wear either a light weight wet suit or no flotation. They do this because they know what they are doing and what their boat driver is doing, but mainly because they need extra freedom of movement for competitive runs. Until you reach this stage always keep the vest on.

Trick Rope

The most important rope characteristic is tautness. A rope that does not stretch gives a steady pull without any sudden jerks. A taut rope is also a safe rope since it does not tend to snap back and coil around an arm or leg.

The optimal trick rope is made of 3/8" braided polypropylene. Variations to this are an official polypropylene slalom line or any rope that possesses a steady, even and strong pull. The standard 75 foot ski line is a good rope for the beginning trick skier to start with. Shortening this rope to 50 feet helps decrease the time intervals between falling and getting back on top of the water, by eliminating 25 feet of unnecessary and cumbersome rope. It also helps prepare the beginning skier for the shorter rope lengths that are necessary for wake tricks.

Selecting the proper rope length is a personal choice that partly depends on the type of boat, the boat speed, the ski design, and the skier's weight. If you are skiing at the average speed of 15 mph, your rope length should be approximately 45 feet long. Adjust the rope length from this point by keeping in mind that the reasons for having a shorter rope length are: to find a flat area between the wakes for doing surface turns, to have a place where the wakes are crisp for wake tricks and to have a place where little time is wasted cutting for the wakes on wake tricks.

Rope Length Considerations

1. Outboards and inboard/outboards generally require a shorter rope than inboards.
2. Narrow skis, heavy skiers and grooved skis require faster speeds which necessitate a longer rope.
3. Use common sense to help as a final judge for determining rope length. If you are wasting time cutting back and forth to position yourself for wake turns, your rope is probably too long. On the other hand, if every time you try a surface turn, you end up in the wakes, your rope is probably too short.

Bear Trap

Trick Handles and Toe Straps

The trick handle should be a standard 11½″ long. Longer handles are available but the larger size makes them more cumbersome than useful.

There are a variety of toehold straps that can be used. The best ones are usually made of canvas. Rubber and leather straps are also available but generally do not hold onto your foot or hold together as well as canvas.

Deciding between using a sling, a toe strap that doesn't close on your foot, and a bear trap, a strap that does close on your foot, depends on your skiing ability. If you have just started to learn toeholds, a sling is the better strap. This strap comes off your foot as soon as you start to fall; a comforting thought to the skier who is apprehensive about toehold turns. If you are making the toe front to back, back to front and the wake toe turns, you should use a bear trap. This strap stays on your foot and helps eliminate unnecessary falls; a necessity for the competitor who plans on doing more than the basic toe turns.

Sling

Trick Rope Release

A trick rope release is a safety devise that every trick skier should consider using, especially when doing reverse toe turns. It is designed to release the rope from the boat, thus eliminating or at least reducing the possibilities of dragging in the water after a fall. However, trick rope releases are only as good as the person who operates them and ultimately it is the skier's responsibility to be able to get out of bad situations without the release. Use common sense when employing a release, don't rely on it, use it as a back up.

Boat

One particular nice thing about trick skiing is almost any boat that can pull a skier up to 20 mph can be used. In most cases the actual preparation of the boat can be more important than the boat design. Consider the following when preparing your boat for trick skiing.
1. Use a large ski mirror that allows the driver to watch for falls and to see what the skier is doing on the water.
2. Use a speedometer that is large enough to read and is sensitive enough to denote ¼ mph changes in speed.
3. Adjust the engine tilt on an outboard or inboard/ outboard so the boat is planed at trick skiing speeds. This is accomplished by moving the engine tilt in or down. A trick speed is easier to maintain when the boat is planed.
4. Level the boat wakes. Uneven boat wakes require the use of cement blocks, sand bags or readjustment of the boat crew to make the wakes level. A level boat makes a better wake for tricks and is easier to drive.

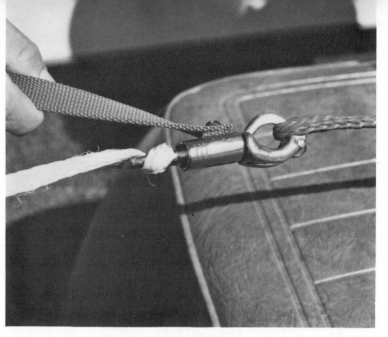

Trick rope releases are only as good as the person who operates them. Don't rely on it, use it as a back up.

RIDING TRICK SKIS FOR THE FIRST TIME

Your first time on a pair of trick skis is going to be different than any other skiing you have done. At first the skis might feel unsteady, a little wobbly. Don't be concerned, they begin to feel comfortable as you ski more.

Initially set the boat speed at about 15 mph. If the skis are unstable, go slower until they feel comfortable. On the other hand, if the skis are dragging and impossible to maneuver, then speed up. At slow speeds the skis drag more and are more controllable, while at fast speeds the skis plane higher and turn easier.

Continue skiing until you feel comfortable and confident on the trick skis. Once stability has been achieved, start playing on the skis. Begin by crossing and jumping the wakes. Then try to break the skis from their forward plane by hopping slightly and turning the skis with your ankles.

Setting the Boat Speed

Setting the boat speed is the skier's responsibility. The boat speed must be fast enough to allow the skis to turn and yet slow enough to give control. But most importantly, the speed must feel comfortable.

Place yourself into one of the following categories and set a speed in that range. Keep in mind that a heavy weight skier, narrow skis, grooved skis and a long rope generally require faster speeds. Also note that a faster speed is required for skiing on one ski.

1. **8 to 12 mph.** A speed for small children. (Under 100 lbs.)
2. **13 to 17 mph.** The speed for most skiers. (100-180 lbs.)
3. **Over 17 mph.** Speeds for very heavy skiers. (Over 180 lbs.)

TRICK SKIING FUNDAMENTALS

Learning to trick ski is actually learning to control basic fundamentals on the water. These fundamentals are simple and when adhered to, result in rapid trick development.

1. Rotate your trick smoothly and slowly.
2. Use your natural body position. Keep your head up, knees and arms slightly bent and shoulders level.
3. Keep the handle in at your waist during all arm tricks; likewise keep your toehold foot in on all toe turns.
4. Let the boat wake do most of the work for you on wake tricks.
5. Relax!

Regardless of your skill, successful trick skiing is accomplished by mastering these fundamentals. Almost every fall or mistake is the result of not adhering to one or more of these. Know these fundamentals and use them.

Surface Turns

Basic surface turns are simple tricks. The key to learning them is remembering that surface turns need to be rotated smoothly and slowly. Always bend your knees, keep your head up and the handle in at your waist.

The two most common falls are falling towards the boat while skiing backwards and having the skis stop during rotation. If you find yourself falling toward the boat look for two errors: either the handle has gotten away from your body or your body is too erect and stiff. If your skis are stopping during rotation, look for three possible errors: first, you are spinning too fast, second, your head may be down during the trick, and third, the handle has strayed away from your body.

Wake Turns

Wake turns use the same basic principles as surface turns, with some other considerations added. The keys to successful execution are: letting the boat wake do the work for you, starting the turn at the peak of the wake (top), keeping the handle at your waist during the entire trick, keeping your head up, spinning the turn and passing, not throwing, the handle from hand to hand.

Most people have the mistaken notion that it takes a giant leap at the top of the wake to successfully complete a wake trick. Actually a big push has a tendency to push the skis into the wake and stop ski rotation. When learning wake tricks, concentrate on spinning and passing the handle near the body. Don't worry about clearance until you have mastered the mechanics of the trick.

The most common falls on wake tricks are caused by letting the handle get out away from the body. Any time the handle is not close to your waist you will get stretched out. That is, your arms will be straightened and you will be pulled toward the boat. Keep the handle near your waist during all wake tricks.

Another common error is turning before you reach the peak of the wake. This problem becomes apparent quickly because the skis normally stop at the start of the rotation, resulting in a quick, hard fall. The same type of fall can result from looking down. Always keep your head up and wait for the peak of the wake before initiating your turn.

Stepover Turns

To many skiers, stepover turns are the most unusual tricks they try. The key to doing stepovers is believing you can make them.

The most challenging part of a stepover is getting your ski, or free leg to go over the rope. To accomplish this, pull the rope in, keep both your stepover and ski leg bent, and throw the stepover leg over the rope while turning.

The most common fall is leaning away from the boat. This is usually caused by not bending the ski leg and by not having the handle in during the turn. Always keep the handle near your waist and your stepover and ski leg bent.

Photo Spray Publications, Inc.

Toe Turns

Toe turns can be the easiest tricks you try. However, like stepovers, toe turns can be more difficult to mentally accept than to perform. The most important thing to remember is that toe turns can be done easily and safely.

To initiate the turn, bend your ski leg and give a slight hop. During the turn keep your shoulders level, your toehold foot in and your ski leg bent.

The most common error is falling away from the boat on the toe back to front. This fall is caused either by letting the toehold leg straighten or by having the upper body too far back when coming frontward. Always keep the toehold foot in and reach over the front of the ski as you are turning frontward.

Learn toe turns with a sling or bear trap you know will come off. Putting the strap on your toes instead of all the way up your foot allows the strap to come off easily during a fall and makes learning more comfortable and safer.

THE TRICK GUIDE

In the illustrated instructions to follow, tricks have been placed in a recommended order of learning. The guide consists of six groups of tricks, each group representing elevated stages in a trick skier's development.

Ideally a skier starts in group one, works down the list, and then goes on to the next group. However, the trick schedule is not meant to be rigid, the purpose of it is to guide. You must always remember that each person learns at a different rate and has different strengths and weaknesses. It is to your advantage to constantly try new tricks so you can exploit your strengths to their maximum potential. Because the guide suggests waiting to try a new trick is no reason to refrain from it. If you have the urge and believe a trick can be attempted safely, then do it.

You will immediately notice that two ski tricks are almost completely neglected from the guide. Generally two ski tricks are more difficult to perfect than one ski tricks and have lower competitive point values. Also, two ski tricks are not closely correlated to their one ski counterparts and are not necessary for advancement to the one ski tricks.

Before going through the guide look through the following list of suggestions. Adherence to these basics can speed up your learning.

1. Rotate your tricks smoothly and slowly.
2. Maintain a natural body position. Keep your head up and knees and arms bent.
3. Relax.
4. Keep the handle near your waist during all arm tricks.
5. Keep your toehold foot in during all toe turn tricks.
6. Let the wake do most of the work on wake tricks.
7. Be natural, let your body respond to what you are attempting.
8. Visualize yourself doing a trick before you attempt it. Imagine yourself on the water doing it and skiing away from it.
9. Prepare yourself for a trick. If a trick requires a wrap or some special preparation, know how to do it before you ski.
10. Have confidence in your ability to learn quickly.
11. Always work on one or two new tricks during a practice session.

Rick McCormick performs a wake stepover 360.

GROUP I

TWO SKIS
Side Slide
Front to Back
Back to Front
Reverse Front to Back
Reverse Back to Front
360
Wake Front to Back
Wake Back to Front
Wake 360 Wrap
Wake 360
Stepover Back to Front
Stepover Front to Back

GROUP II

ONE SKI
Side Slide
Front to Back
Back to Front
Reverse Front to Back
Reverse Back to Front
360
Reverse 360
Wake Front to Back
Wake Back to Front

GROUP III

ONE SKI (cont.)
Toehold Front to Back
Toehold Back to Front
Toehold Wake Front to Back
Toehold Wake Back to Front
Wake 360
Reverse Wake 360
Stepover Front to Back
Stepover Back to Front

GROUP IV

ONE SKI (cont.)
Wake Stepover Front to Back
Wake Stepover Back to Front
Back Wrap Position
Wake Back to Back
Reverse Wake Back to Back
Wake Stepover 360 Wrap
Wake Stepover 360
Reverse Wake Stepover 360

GROUP V

ONE SKI (cont.)
Toehold Wake 360 Wrap
Toehold Wake 360
Wake 540 Back to Front
Wake 540 Front to Back
Reverse Toehold Front to Back
Reverse Toehold Back to Front
Toehold Back to Back
Reverse Toehold Back to Back

GROUP VI

ONE SKI (cont.)
Toehold 540 Front to Back
Toehold 360
Reverse Toehold 360
Toehold Wake Back to Back
Reverse Wake 540 Back to Front
Reverse Wake 540 Front to Back
Wake Stepover 540 Back to Front

GROUP I

TWO SKI TRICKS

Side Slide

1. Pull the handle in to your waist.
2. Initiate a turn to the left with a slight hop and a turn of your shoulders.
3. Lean slightly away from the boat in the side slide position.

KEY: Break the forward plane of the skis with a slight hop.

Front to Back

1. Pull the handle in to your waist.
2. Initiate a turn to the left with a slight hop and a turn of your head.
3. Release your left hand from the handle.
4. Grab the handle with your left hand as you complete the turn.

KEY: Keep the handle near your body during the turn.

Back to Front

1. Initiate a turn to the right with a turn of your head.
2. Release your left hand from the handle.
3. Quickly grab the handle with your left hand while turning frontward.

KEY: Quickly grab the handle with your left hand.

1

2

3

Reverse Front to Back and Reverse Back to Front

1. Same procedure as FB and BF, only substitute right for left and left for right.

360 Degree Turn

1. The first half of the turn is the same as the FB.
2. In the back position continue turning to the left and release your right hand from the handle.
3. Grab the handle with your right hand while turning frontward.

KEY: Keep the handle near your body in the back position.

1

2

3

4

5

Wake Front to Back

1. From the middle of the wakes, moderately cut to the left at about a 30 degree angle.
2. At the top of the wake, straighten your legs, initiate a turn to the left with a turn of your head and release your left hand from the handle.
3. Grab the handle with your left hand as you complete the turn.
4. Land with your knees bent and the handle near your body.

KEY: Keep the handle near your body at the start of the turn.

Wake Back to Front

1. Remain in the back position established by the wake back.
2. Moderately cut back to the wake at about a 30 degree angle.
3. At the top of the wake, straighten your legs, initiate a turn to the right with a turn of your head and release your left hand from the handle.
4. Grab the handle with your left hand while turning frontward.
5. Land with your knees bent and the handle near your body.

KEY: Keep the handle near your body on the landing.

Wake 360 Wrap (shown at right)

1. Hold the handle vertically and straight out from your body.
2. Pull the handle in to your right side and release your left hand from the handle.
3. Quickly reach your left hand around your back and grab the handle.
4. Release your right hand from the handle and place it on the rope in front of the bridle.

KEY: Quickly grab the handle with your left hand.

1

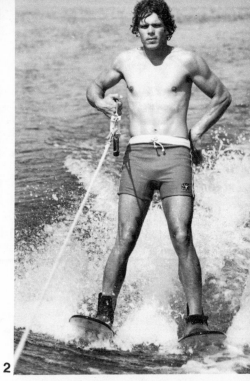

2

3

4

Wake 360

1. Attain the WO wrap position.
2. Ski about five feet outside the right boat wake.
3. Moderately cut to the wake at about a 30 degree angle.
4. At the top of the wake, straighten your legs, initiate a turn to the left with a turn of your head and release your right hand from the rope.
5. During the turn keep the handle near your body.
6. Grab the handle with your right hand while turning frontward.
7. Land with your knees bent and the handle near your body.

KEY: Keep the handle near your body during the entire turn and initiate the turn after you leave the wake.

1

2

3

Stepover Back to Front

1. Attain the back position.
2. Hold the handle between your legs with your left hand and use your right arm for balance.
3. Lift the left ski out of the water by bending your left leg.
4. Initiate a turn to the left with a hop and a turn of your head.
5. Lift your leg over the rope during the turn.
6. Grab the handle with your right hand as you complete the turn.

KEY: Lift the ski over the rope.

Stepover Front to Back

1. Pull the rope in to your waist.
2. Lift your left ski out of the water by bending your left leg.
3. Initiate a turn to the right with a hop and a turn of your head.
4. Throw your left leg over the rope and release your right hand from the handle during the turn.
5. In the back position use your right arm for balance.

KEY: Force the ski over the rope.

GROUP II

ONE SKI TRICKS

The illustrated one ski tricks to follow are for a right foot forward skier. If you are a left foot forward skier, substitute right for left and left for right for all wake tricks. On surface tricks, turn in the direction that feels natural and gives you the most control.

Side Slide
1. Pull the handle in to your waist.
2. Initiate a turn to the left with a slight hop and turn of your shoulders.
3. Lean slightly away from the boat in the side slide position.

KEY: Break the forward plane of the ski with a slight hop.

3

4

1   2

Front to Back (*shown here*)
1. Pull the handle in to your waist.
2. Initiate a turn to the left with a slight hop and a turn of your head.
3. Release your left hand from the handle.
4. Grab the handle with your left hand as you complete the turn.

KEY: Keep the handle near your body.

| 1 | 2 | 3 | 4 |

Back to Front (shown above)

1. Initiate a turn to the right with a turn of your head.
2. Release your left hand from the handle.
3. Quickly grab the handle with your left hand while turning frontward.

KEY: Quickly grab the handle with your left hand.

Reverse Front to Back and Reverse Back to Front

1. Same procedure as FB and BF, only substitute right for left and left for right.

360 Degree Turn

1. The first half of the turn is the same as the FB.
2. In the back position continue turning to the right and release your right hand from the handle.
3. Grab the handle with your left hand while turning frontward.

KEY: Keep the handle near your body.

Reverse 360 Degree Turn

1. Same procedure as 360, only substitute right for left and left for right.

Wake Front to Back (below)

1. From the middle of the wakes, moderately cut to the left at about a 30 degree angle.
2. At the top of the wake, straighten your legs, initiate a turn to the left with a turn of your head and release your left hand from the handle.
3. Grab the handle with your left hand as you complete the turn.
4. Land with your knees bent and the handle near your body.

KEY: Keep the handle near your body at the start of the turn.

Wake Back to Front (above)

1. Remain in the back position as established by the WB.
2. Moderately cut back to the wake at about a 30 degree angle.
3. At the top of the wake, straighten your legs, initiate a turn to the right with a turn of your head and release your left hand from the handle.
4. Grab the handle with your left hand while turning frontward.
5. Land with your knees bent and the handle near your body.

KEY: Keep the handle near your body on the landing.

GROUP III

ONE SKI TRICKS (cont.)

Toehold Front to Back

1. Place your left foot in the toehold strap and bend your ski leg.
2. Pull your toehold leg in and initiate a turn to the right with a slight hop and a turn of your head.
3. Keep your shoulders level and use your arms for balance.

KEY: Keep your shoulders level.

1

2

3

4

1

2

Toehold Back to Front
1. Bend your ski leg.
2. Pull your toehold leg in and initiate a turn to the left with a slight hop and a turn of your head.
3. Reach forward with your right arm while turning frontward.

KEY: Reach forward while turning frontward.

3

4

Toehold Wake Front to Back

1. From the middle of the wakes, moderately cut to the right at about a 30 degree angle.
2. At the top of the wake, straighten your ski leg, pull your toehold leg in and initiate a turn to the right with a turn of your head.
3. Land with your ski leg bent and your shoulders level.

KEY: Keep your shoulders level.

1

2

3

4

1

2

3

Toehold Wake Back to Front

1. Remain in the back position established by the TWB.
2. Moderately cut back to the wake at about a 30 degree angle.
3. At the top of the wake, straighten your ski leg, pull your toehold leg in and initiate a turn to the left with a turn of your head.
4. Reach forward with your right arm while turning frontward.
5. Land with your ski leg bent and your shoulders level.

KEY: Reach forward while turning frontward.

4

Wake 360 *(below)*

1. Attain the WO wrap position.
2. Ski about five feet outside the right boat wake.
3. Moderately cut to the wake at about a 30 degree angle.
4. At the top of the wake, straighten your legs, initiate a turn to the left with a turn of your head and release your right hand from the rope.
5. During the turn keep the handle near your body.
6. Grab the handle with your right hand while turning frontward.
7. Land with your knees bent and the handle near your body.

KEY: Keep the handle near your body.

Reverse Wake 360 *(above)*

1. Same procedure as wake 360, only substitute right for left and left for right on the WO wrap and WO.

Stepover Back to Front (below)

1. Remain in the back position established by the stepover front to back.
2. Bend your stepover leg.
3. Initiate a turn to the left with a hop and a turn of your head.
4. Lift your stepover leg over the rope during the turn.
5. Grab the handle with your right hand as you complete the turn.

KEY: Keep the handle close to your body.

Stepover Front to Back (above)

1. Pull the rope in to your waist.
2. Bend your stepover leg.
3. Initiate a turn to the right with a hop and a turn of your head.
4. Lift your stepover leg over the rope and release your right hand from the handle.
5. In the back position use your right arm for balance.

KEY: Keep the handle near your body.

GROUP IV

ONE SKI TRICKS (cont.)

Wake Stepover Front to Back
1. From the middle of the wakes, moderately cut to the left at about a 30 degree angle.
2. Before reaching the wake, bend your stepover leg.
3. At the top of the wake, pull the handle in to your waist, straighten your ski leg and initiate a turn to the right with a turn of your head.
4. As you turn, lift your stepover leg over the rope and release your right hand from the handle.
5. Land with your ski leg bent and use your right arm for balance.

KEY: Land with your shoulders level.

1

2

3

4

Wake Stepover Back to Front (*below*)

1. Remain in the back position established by the WLB.
2. Moderately cut back to the wake at about a 30 degree angle.
3. Before reaching the wake, bend your stepover leg.
4. At the top of the wake, straighten your ski leg and initiate a turn to the left with a turn of your head.
5. As you turn frontward grab the handle with your right hand.
6. Land with your ski leg bent and the handle near your body.

KEY: Land with the handle near your body.

Back Wrap (*above*)

1. Pull the handle in to your waist.
2. Initiate a turn to the right with your shoulders while looking at the boat.
3. Force the ski to remain backwards by holding the handle next to your waist.

KEY: Force the ski to remain backwards.

1

2

Wake Back to Back
1. Attain the back wrap position.
2. From the middle of the wakes, moderately cut to the left at about a 30 degree angle.
3. At the top of the wake, straighten your legs, and initiate a turn to the left with a turn of your shoulders.
4. During the first 180 degree turn keep both hands on the handle.
5. Release your left hand from the handle in the front position.
6. Quickly grab the handle with your left hand as you complete the turn.
7. Land with your knees bent and the handle near your body.

KEY: Let the wake do the work.

3

Reverse Wake Back to Back (*below*)

1. Remain in the back position established by the WBB.
2. Moderately cut back to the wake at about a 30 degree angle.
3. At the top of the wake, straighten your legs, initiate a turn to the right with a turn of your head and release your left hand from the handle.
4. Grab the handle with your left hand as you come to the front position.
5. Complete the turn to the back position with both hands on the handle.
6. Land in the back wrap position with your knees bent and the handle next to your waist.

KEY: Land with the handle next to your waist.

Wake Stepover 360 Wrap (*above*)

1. Pull the handle in to the right side of your right knee.
2. Release your left hand from the handle and quickly reach behind your right knee.
3. Grab the handle with your left hand.
4. Release your right hand from the handle and place it on the rope in front of the bridle.

KEY: Keep your weight on the front of the ski.

Wake Stepover 360 (below)

1. Attain the WLO wrap.
2. From the middle of the wakes, moderately cut to the left at about a 30 degree angle.
3. At the top of the wake straighten your ski leg, initiate a turn to the left with a turn of your head and release your right hand from the rope.
4. During the turn keep the handle near your knee and your shoulders level.
5. As you turn frontward, lift your leg over the rope and reach forward with your right hand and grab the handle.
6. Land with your ski leg bent and the handle near your waist.

KEY: Keep your shoulders level and reach forward with your right arm.

Reverse Wake Stepover 360 (above)

1. Ski about five feet outside the left wake.
2. Approach the trick like a WLB only push harder off the wake.
3. In the back position quickly grab the handle with your right hand on the outside of your right leg.
4. Release your left hand from the handle in the back position.
5. As you turn frontward grab the handle with your left hand.
6. Land with your ski leg bent and the handle close to your body.

KEY: Quickly grab the handle in the back position.

GROUP V

ONE SKI TRICKS (cont.)

Toehold 360 Wrap

1. Pull the handle in to your waist with both hands.
2. Release your left hand from the handle and grab the rope in front of the bridle.
3. Pull the rope in with your left hand so there is no pull on the handle.
4. Move your left leg behind your right knee.
5. Put the toehold strap on your foot with your right hand.
6. Turn the strap so the open end is up.
7. Release your right hand from the handle and place it in front of your left hand.

KEY: Before attempting it do the technique on shore.

1

2

3

Toehold Wake 360 *(shown here)*

1. Ski about five feet outside the right boat wake.
2. Attain the TO wrap position.
3. Moderately cut to the wake at about a 30 degree angle.
4. At the top of the wake, straighten your ski leg, initiate a turn to the left with a turn of your head and release your hands from the rope.
5. During the turn keep your left knee (toehold leg) and your right knee (ski leg) close together.
6. Reach forward with your right arm as you complete the turn.
7. Land with both legs bent and your shoulders level.

KEY: Keep your left knee close to your right knee during the entire trick.

3

4

1

2

Wake 540 Back to Front

1. Attain the back wrap position.
2. From the middle of the wakes, moderately cut to the left at about a 30 degree angle.
3. At the top of the wake, straighten your legs and initiate a turn to the left with a turn of your head.
4. During the first 180 degree turn keep both hands on the handle.
5. In the front position release your left hand from the handle.
6. Grab the handle with your left hand as you complete the turn backward, then release your right hand from the handle.
7. Grab the handle with your right hand as you complete the turn frontward.
8. Land with your knees bent, your shoulders level and the handle near your body.

KEY: Keep your shoulders level.

Wake 540 Front to Back

1. Ski about five feet outside the left wake.
2. Moderately cut to the wake at about a 30 degree angle.
3. At the top of the wake, straighten your legs, pull the handle in to your left hip, initiate a turn to the right with a turn of your head and release your right hand from the handle.
4. Grab the handle with your right hand as you complete the turn backward and release your left hand from the handle.
5. Grab the handle with your left hand as you complete the turn frontward.
6. Turn backward with both hands on the handle.
7. Land in the back wrap position, with your knees bent and the handle next to your waist.

KEY: Keep the handle near your body.

1

2

3

4

5

Reverse Toehold Front to Back

1. Bend your ski leg.
2. Pull your toehold leg in.
3. Initiate a turn to the left with a slight hop and a turn of your shoulders.
4. During the turn keep your shoulders level and your ski leg bent.
5. Prepare to come frontward.

KEY: Keep your shoulders level and your ski leg bent.

Reverse Toehold Back to Front

1. Keep your toehold leg in and your ski leg bent.
2. Initiate the turn frontward with a turn of your shoulders.
3. During the turn reach forward with your left arm.

KEY: Reach forward while turning.

1 2

3 4 5

Reverse Toehold Back to Back (*below*)
1. Attain the TB position.
2. Slowly turn to the front position by keeping your toehold leg in.
3. Continue turning past the front position by pulling with your toehold leg and leading the turn with your shoulders.
4. During the turn backward keep your shoulders level and your ski leg bent.

KEY: Turn the ski slowly and keep your shoulders level going in to the RTB position.

Toehold Back to Back (*above*)
1. Attain RTB position.
2. Slowly slide to the TF position by keeping your toehold leg in.
3. Continue turning past the front position by pulling your toehold leg in.
4. Slowly turn to the TB position.

KEY: Keep your toehold leg in and turn slowly to the TF position.

GROUP VI

ONE SKI TRICKS (cont.)

Toehold 540 Front to Back
KEY: Maintain a smooth and slow ski rotation, keep
your shoulders level and your toehold foot near
your ski leg during the entire turn.

3

1

2

Toehold 360 (below)

KEY: Keep your toehold foot near your ski leg and your shoulders level during the turn.

Reverse Toehold 360 (wrap in)

KEY: Reach forward with your left hand as you turn frontward.

Toehold Wake Back to Back
KEY: Keep your toehold foot near your ski leg during the turn and rotate the trick slowly.

Photo Rick McCormick

Reverse Wake 540 Back to Front
KEY: Become comfortable in the reverse back wrap position and keep the handle near your waist during the turn.

Reverse Wake 540 Front to Back
KEY: Keep the handle near your waist during the entire turn.

Wake Stepover 540 Back to Front
KEY: Use ear plugs.

THE TRICK RUN

A great deal of personal judgement is required in performing a trick run since there are no required tricks. All skiers must determine for themselves what tricks they wish to do, in what order the tricks will be performed at what pace to ski and how to practice the run.

Which Tricks to Use

The trick run dilemma is that a skier has only two 20-second passes to score points. Often you must make the tradeoff between a desire for more points and a risk of falling on unperfected tricks. The philosophies vary from doing many easy tricks and building points slowly to doing a series of a few high point tricks. Most skiers use a compromise of these two philosophies.

Deciding which tricks to use is the biggest decision you have to make because some tricks become more consistent than others. In determining which tricks to use, evaluate what your trick run goal is. For instance, if the goal is a certain number of points or beating a competitor's run, and doing this requires doing some inconsistent tricks, then they must be used. Or if working on a future run requires some experimenting, then taking risks in a few tournaments may be required. The same principle applies in the other direction. If there is an immediate goal to reach, but that goal doesn't require taking chances, then refrain from taking those chances. Only you can decide what you want and need from a trick run. Establish a goal and set the run accordingly.

Trick Order

The first trick of each pass is the most critical. Successful execution of it can help set a good pace for the entire trick run. Select a first trick that you have confidence in; a trick you know you will make.

All your tricks, including the first, should be placed in sequences; toeholds with toeholds, stepovers with stepovers, wake tricks with wake tricks and surface turns with surface turns. Placing similiar tricks together insures continuity in thinking (not confusing different kinds of tricks) and is logical. For instance, putting a foot in and out of a toe strap can waste valuable time in a trick turn.

Pace

Speed in a run is necessary to do more tricks and accumulate more points. This speed is established by smoothness and proper execution of each trick, not by rushing. Attempts at rushing the tempo usually result in bobbles that either slow you down or cause a fall. Place your tricks in a good sequence and concentrate on properly executing each trick, one at a time, and the speed will take care of itself.

PRACTICE

The key to becoming a good trick skier is getting on the water to learn new tricks. In that sense there is no such thing as too much practice in trick skiing. However the amount of practice time you spend depends on what your skiing goals are and the time constraints you are skiing under.

The best form of daily trick skiing practice consists of a series of three to four 15 minute sessions. These relatively short sessions keep you physically and mentally fresh. In each session pick one or two tricks to work on and give them your complete physical and mental attention. Establish a pattern in each session for practicing those tricks and stay with it.

At the same time, allow some flexibility in this schedule to try new tricks and different techniques. Saving a few minutes each day for new tricks might result in learning a trick you thought was too difficult.

Try to use the same boat driver for each practice session. Having someone who knows your speeds and habits can save time and make practice sessions more beneficial.

Finally make your trick practice meaningful. Don't perform for the boat crew, work on your tricks. Use a driver and an observer who will not be distracting.

Practice Attitude

Many people approach trick skiing with the attitude that it is difficult and too time consuming. Actually trick skiing is easy when approached with the proper instruction, equipment and a positive learning attitude.

When you decide you are going to become a trick skier, do it with the idea that you can easily learn each trick you try. Approach a new trick with a relaxed confidence that you can make it and eliminate any pre-attempt prejudice on the difficulty of the trick.

Use the "no fall" philosophy. Do everything you can to stand up on a new trick. For example, on wake tricks try sliding the ski over the wake or breaking the trick into parts. A wake 360 can be done as a wake FB 180 and a surface BF 180 turning in the same direction. On surface turns of 360 degrees or more break the trick into 180 degree turns. Concentrate on completing a new trick from start to finish and then begin to perfect it.

Constantly try new tricks. The old idea of mastering a trick before moving on to new tricks does not stand up today. The "mastering of old tricks process" is too slow and implies correlations between tricks that usually don't exist.

Develop the ability to analyze your trick skiing mistakes. Learn to control your body movements with your mind and make the mental and physical adjustments necessary to do tricks correctly. But don't restrict yourself by becoming overly critical of every body movement you make or think you have made.

Limit your analysis to the basics: smooth trick rotation, natural body position, handle in, etc.

At the same time learn to accept some mistakes and falls as just poor attempts caused by lack of experience or practice. These mistakes and falls generally disappear and need not be analyzed except when they persist.

Photo Rick McCormick

Finally avoid making the mistake of placing a time period on how long a trick will take to learn. There simply is no way of knowing how long a trick takes to develop since each person and each trick has different characteristics. Saying a trick will take a month to make or a year to learn will quite often talk you into taking that long. Approach each trick with the attitude that you are going to make it immediately, but accept it when you have to spend time working on it.

Practicing the Run

Practice a trick run with the same attitude you have in competition; set your goal at making that run. Concentrate on avoiding the careless habits of rushing tempo, dropping the handle or falling on tricks that are not difficult for you. These repetitive kinds of practice mistakes are the usual causes of tournament falls. Use your head in practice and avoid tournament disappointments.

Divide your practice time between learning new tricks and perfecting trick runs based on your ability and ski goals. Beginning trick skiers should spend most of their time learning new tricks while good overall skiers need to spend most of their time making their trick runs consistent. Knowing how much time you must spend on learning new tricks and practicing trick runs becomes more apparent as you compete. The time breakdown depends on the consistency of your trick run, your competitor's run and your desires to improve your run.

A final point to consider is that a given trick run is only advantageous for a short period of time. Your preoccupation with learning new tricks and for improving your trick run should make you want to always improve your run. Don't stay with the same run. It's a quick way to slow your learning and lose your trick skiing interest.

COMPETITION

The most important pre-trick run preparation before competition is relaxing. Before you ski, gain complete control of your mind by learning to mentally isolate yourself from the other tournament activities. Calm yourself so your tricks can be performed like they are done in practice.

Besides gaining mental control you have the responsibility of finding out if the tow boat makes any unusual approach or turn before and during the course. Note, if there is any point in the course where waves are likely to occur and if the boat is driven close to the shoreline, jump or any other object during the run. Your responsibility is to know what is going on before taking to the water. Never be surprised.

Camille Duvall prepares for the first trick of a run.

Photo Rick McCo[r]

Next, prepare for the first trick of each pass. Visualize approximately where you must begin the pre-trick preparation and note where the starting gates are.

When the boat driver comes to pick you up, tell him or her the approximate speed you wish to trick at. As soon as you are skiing, set the speed you desire and begin to loosen up by cutting across the wakes and doing a few basic tricks.

When approaching the course, concentrate on the first trick. If it requires some special preparation or wrapping technique, accomplish it calmly before entering the trick course.

Once into the run you must concentrate on not falling, holding onto the handle and keeping a steady tempo. Perform each trick, one at a time. If you make a mistake don't become flustered, just reestablish your composure and go on.

The capacity to focus your concentration on standing up through your trick run requires discipline. On some days this discipline is more difficult to achieve. When these days occur, concentration can be carried one step farther by verbalizing the three basic points during your run: not falling, holding onto the handle and keeping a steady tempo. Talk yourself into making your run.

ADVERSE WATER CONDITIONS

Competition trick skiing under adverse water conditions is not common. The fact that a trick course is often right next to the shore usually offers enough protection from windy conditions. Also, because the skier is close to the boat, the boat will absorb most of the waves before they reach the skier.

However, when conditions are adverse, slow down your tempo and increase your concentration on standing up. Don't take chances. Accept the fact that you must slow down to reach your number one objective of not falling.

DRIVING

As a trick driver you have four major driving requirements. You must find the desired speed, maintain that speed, drive in a straight line and get the boat back quickly to a fallen skier.

Finding the desired speed is partly the responsibility of the skier. As a driver, you can help by asking the skier approximately what speed he or she wants and then getting to that speed as quickly as possible. From there it is up to the skier to signify the speed adjustments that are necessary.

To help maintain the set speed, always hold your hand on the throttle. As you feel the speed change or see the speedometer move, adjust the throttle accordingly with smooth, gradual movements. Keep the speedometer on the same reading and learn to anticipate and compensate for the skier's pull.

Sometimes your preoccupation with holding the speed, watching for other boats and watching the skier can make driving in a straight line difficult. Occasionally glance in the mirror to see if the boat has traveled in a straight path. If it has not, adjust the wheel; aim for some distant shore maker and stay on that course.

One of the most important driving functions is to quickly get the boat back to the skier after each fall. This helps keep the skier from getting cold and helps maintain his or her enthusiasm. When the skier does fall, immediately stop the boat and make sure the skier is clear of the rope and OK. If the skier does not need assistance, make a small radius turn and come back to the skier in the same path the boat has traveled. This type of turn keeps boat waves from going through the practice area.

JUMPING

Jumping is the spectacular water skiing event. In fact, one of the most exciting sights in all sports is to see a highly skilled water ski jumper cutting across the water at nearly 70 mph and then soaring 170 feet or farther off a water ski jump.

After witnessing a jumper of this caliber most people are surprised that learning to jump is easy. With proper instruction and equipment almost anyone who can ride two skis can quickly and safely learn how to do it.

However after learning the basics, most beginning jumpers are not content with just skiing over the ramp. They have the desire to fly farther on each jump they take. They wish to be long distance jumpers.

To become a long distance jumper a skier must build extra speed on the approach to the ramp and then push off the top of the jump. Initially the extra speed is generated by increasing the speed of the boat to the maximum allowed for the jumper's division *(see appendix)*. After this speed is reached, more speed is attained by using the double wake cut. It's only through the successful combination of the cut and spring that a skier maximizes jump distances.

Jumping requires diligent practice to achieve the precision cut/spring timing for long distance jumps. It also requires a special spirit to do what some people will not do: push on. This special spirit, along with a desire to know how far you fly and a passion to fly farther than anyone else, makes jumping a natural competitive event.

In tournaments a jumper is given three opportunities to go over the ramp. The skier may jump on one, two or all three of the attempts, but only the longest jump is scored. The skier with the longest jump wins.

JUMP RAMP AND COURSE

The standard jump ramp is 14 feet wide and 24 feet long. The height is always adjustable from five to six feet and sometimes adjustable to four feet or less for beginning jumpers.

The jump deck (surface) is generally constructed of 3/4" plywood fastened to a reinforced wood or steel framework. A fiberglass or hard wax coating makes the jump surface smooth and slippery. During use water needs to run over the entire deck to cool the wax and lubricate the surface.

The jump deck framework is hinged to a wood or steel undercarriage that is floated by 55 gallon steel drums or some other form of adequate flotation. Attached to each side of the deck are side boards, also called side curtains. The purpose of these side boards is to prevent a jumper from skiing into the undercarriage area of the jump on a miscalculated double wake cut. Though seldomly needed, the side boards are one safety requirement that should not be neglected.

Jump ramps are commonly anchored with four 3/4"

ropes or steel cables; one tied to each of the four corners of the jump. The ropes or cables are crisscrossed and anchored by heavy weights or screw anchors. The anchor lines are pulled tight so the jump will not change angles from the wind or boat wakes.

The jump course is approximately 800 feet long and comprised of the jump, two boat guide buoys, two timing buoys, a skier cut buoy and a rideout buoy (see diagram). Both boat guide buoys are placed parallel to the front of the ramp. The first is 45 feet wide of the center line of the ramp and the second is 60 feet wide. The two timing buoys are placed in line with the 45 foot boat guide buoy and spaced 285 feet apart. They are used in competition to time the boat to ensure that the boat speed for each contestant remains within a prescribed tolerance. The skier's cut buoy, referred to as the 500 foot buoy, is anchored 500 feet in front of the jump and gives the skier a counter cut reference point. The rideout buoy is placed 325 feet after the jump. In competition a skier must ski past the rideout buoy to receive credit for a jump.

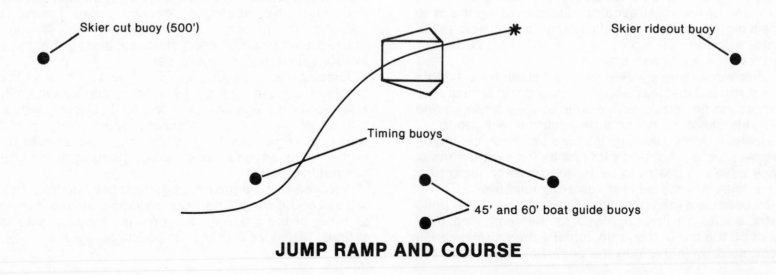

Skier cut buoy (500')

Skier rideout buoy

Timing buoys

45' and 60' boat guide buoys

JUMP RAMP AND COURSE

JUMP SKIS AND EQUIPMENT

The recent development of stronger, longer lasting and safer equipment has contributed to making jumping easier to learn and has dramatically helped improve jump distances. The most significant of these improvements has been the development of fiberglass jump skis. These skis have virtually eliminated structural breakdowns and have given jumpers confidence that their skis will not let them down.

Photo Rick McCormick

Design Characteristics

1. *Large ski tip.* The ski tip should be the same width or wider than the middle width of the ski. The extra ski tip area gives the skis more control, better stability and helps eliminate cutting spray from hitting the skier's face.
2. *Square edges.* The top and bottom edge should be squared for fast acceleration.
3. *Rubber edges.* Rubber edges are an added safety benefit. They also help reduce wear when the skis bang together.
4. *Smooth ski bottom.* The ski bottom must be smooth to achieve maximum acceleration on a double wake cut. Rough ski bottoms can be smoothed with a fine grade of wet/dry sandpaper.
5. *Durable fins.* Fins must be strong, crack resistant and made of a durable wood or plastic.
6. *Moderate ski rocker.* A jump ski should have a moderate rocker from the tail to the tip. The rocker allows the ski to turn easily and ride stably.
7. *Absorbant flexibility.* Jump skis should have a slight amount of flexibility to absorb a good portion of the shock from landings. However, too flexible a ski can accelerate slowly and be uncontrollable in rough water.
8. *Light weight.* Light weight skis are easier to maneuver on top of the water and easier to control in the air.

Construction

Since jump skis take a severe beating and jump ski designs are generally consistent, your most important decision when choosing jump skis will be construction.

1. **Wood.** Wood jump skis can be good for the beginning jumper who does not anticipate competition or who plans on limited jumping sessions. They are the least expensive jump skis but are usually susceptible to rapid wear and breakage.

2. **Fiberglass/foam.** Fiberglass/foam jump skis are used by beginning and recreational jumpers. These skis are light weight, usually more durable than wood skis and moderately priced. However, very few are used by competitiors because they do not offer the strength or stiffness of the more expensive honeycomb or carbon graphite skis.

3. **Fiberglass/aluminum honeycomb and carbon graphite.** Both of these structures are used by serious recreation and competitive jumpers who plan on regular jump sessions. They are light weight, durable and have the stiffness necessary for fast acceleration on double wake cuts.

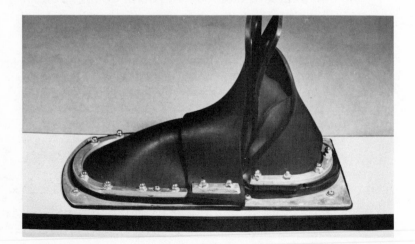

Ski Size

The trend in jump ski sizes has been to use a wider and longer design. Use the following size chart as a guide for choosing the proper length skis, but also check with dealers, competitors and manufacturers' literature for updated sizes.

Skier Size	Ski Length
Children 80 lbs and under	60"
81-100 lbs	66"
101-140 lbs	70"
141 lbs and over	72"

Bindings

Jump bindings should be mounted on an aluminum or strong plastic plate. The main purpose of the plate is to protect the foot if a ski breaks. The plate also spreads the pressure exerted on the binding over a larger ski area, makes binding repair and removal easy and makes changing the binding location relatively simple. Before each jump session check the plate to make sure it is securely attached to the ski.

The binding material must be a strong rubber or nylon reinforced rubber; avoid using hard rubber or plastic. Reinforcement straps around the heel and instep of the foot are necessary for good ski control. The extra support prevents the foot from moving and keeps a tight fit around the ankle. No part of the binding material should extend beyond the bracket. Any loose or uncut pieces of rubber can catch water during a cut and cause a fall.

A rubber pad should be glued on the plate, inside the heel of each binding. This pad softens the impact of landings and protects the heel from stone bruises. The pad should be ¼" to ½" thick and big enough to cushion the heel.

Flotation and Protection

A thick ensolite ski vest is essential for safe jumping. It must fit snugly around the chest to prevent it from riding up on falls and to provide protection. Also, be sure the arm holes are large enough to provide freedom of movement.

Jump pants and wet suit tops are also necessary for protection. The jump pants are especially important for protection on sit-down landings while the wet suit tops offer additional upper body protection.

Ropes and Handles

A 75 foot ski rope is used for jumping. The rope and handle should be made of the same material as used in slalom skiing: ¼" braided polypropylene rope and a rubber coated metal handle. It is very important to pay particular attention to the condition of this equipment. Always check your rope and handle before each session for frays and knots. If the rope or handle is worn, replace it before skiing.

Helmets

The use of a helmet is the personal choice of many jumpers. It offers protection from hitting a ski or the ramp surface on a fall. However, some jumpers are apprehensive about possible neck injuries that could result from the helmet catching water during a fall. If you decide to use a helmet look for the following design characteristics:

1. Light weight plastic construction.
2. Substantial amount of water proof padding inside and on the edges of the helmet.
3. Holes in the top of the helmet to keep it from catching water.
4. A secure double chin strap to keep the helmet from shifting.
5. Easy releasing chin strap buckles.

Arm Slings

An arm sling is used by many advanced competitive jumpers. The purpose of the sling is to improve skier control by holding the right arm near the body during the cut and in the air. However, the sling is not universally used or accepted and the fixed arm position is not beneficial or safe for the beginning or intermediate jumper.

Photo Spray Publications, Inc.

LEARNING TO JUMP

Learning to jump is an exciting experience. The thrill of approaching the jump ramp for the first time and then successfully completing a jump are sensations you will never forget.

Learning to jump is easy and safe when you use the proper equipment and the proper learning procedure.

Equipment

Using the proper jumping equipment includes more than having jump skis, a rope, a vest, etc. It also involves preparing your equipment, the jump ramp and the driver. Before going over the ramp go through the following check list.

1. Always use jump skis. Don't use combination pairs or skis that are not made for jumping.
2. Check the jump skis and fins for cracks and excessive wear.
3. Check the life vest for worn straps and torn shoulders.
4. Check the ski rope for fraying and knots.
5. Check the ramp surface for protruding nails or screws and for excessive wear or warpage.
6. Check the jump approach and landing area for floating objects.
7. Always tighten down any loose anchor lines to securely anchor the ramp.
8. Wet and clean the ramp surface.
9. Use a boat driver who is familiar with pulling beginning jumpers.
10. Review the learning procedure with the driver so each of you are in complete understanding.
11. Use an observer who is aware of the jumping procedure and prepared to offer assistance.

Learning Procedure

Knowing how to control your jump skis before going over the ramp will make learning to jump easier and safer. This ski control is acquired by gaining skiing experience. Ride your jump skis, crossing and jumping the wakes, until you feel comfortable on your skis and you know how they react.

Once you have gained ski control you will be ready to learn to jump. Before you go over the ramp, establish the basic jumping position:

1. Slightly bend your knees.
2. Distribute your weight evenly on both skis.
3. Hold the handle in close at your waist with both hands.
4. Keep your back straight.
5. Hold your head up looking straight ahead at the horizon.
6. Relax!

On your first few jump attempts have the ramp set at five feet. The boat should be driven on the right side at a slight angle to the ramp and the boat speed set based generally on the weight guide below, but also on where you feel comfortable and can control your skis.

Skier's Weight	Approximate Boat Speed
Under 100 lbs	10-15 mph
101-150 lbs	15-20 mph
151-200 lbs	15-25 mph
Over 200 lbs	20-28 mph

As you approach the ramp, pull outside the left boat wake, obtain the basic jumping position and aim your skis for the lower left corner of the ramp (see diagram). When you make contact with the ramp allow the boat to pull you to the right. Concentrate on freezing in the basic jumping position on the jump and in the air.

At the top of the ramp and in the air look straight out at the horizon. Keep both hands on the handle and the handle close to your waist.

Land with your head up and your shoulders level. Absorb the landings with your legs.

Establish the proper basic jumping position before you go over the ramp.

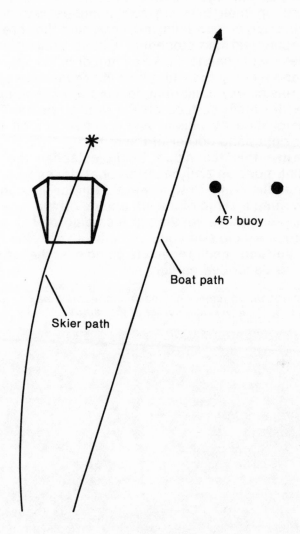

45' buoy

Boat path

Skier path

Beginning skier/driver path

Many beginning jumpers successfully ski away from a jump on their first session. Jumpers who do not, should analyze their falls and make sure they are using the proper learning procedure. Occasionally though, a jumper simply cannot make a jump or is too apprehensive about going over the ramp. For those skiers, there is an easier way of learning to jump without going over the entire jump surface on the first attempts. This is accomplished by skiing over a small portion of the lower right hand corner of the ramp.

To use this technique, again establish the basic jumping position and have the boat driven at a slight angle to the ramp. Now, however, aim for the right side of the ramp instead of the left and go off the lower side of the ramp instead of the top *(see diagram)*. Once you feel comfortable and you can control your skis on the ramp surface, then proceed to going over the top of the ramp as described earlier.

The apprehensive jumper can ease into learning how to jump by skiing over the lower right corner of the ramp.

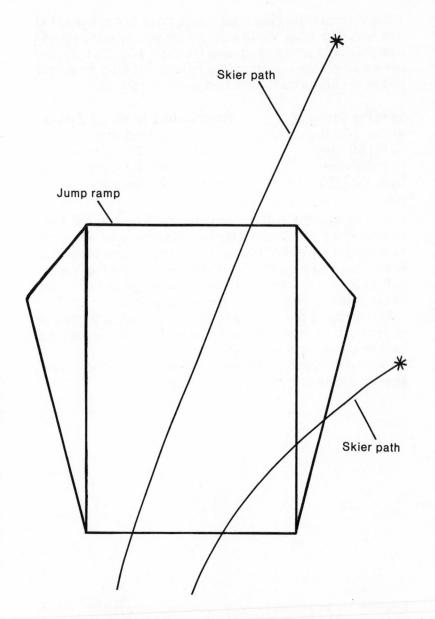

Alternate Learning Procedure

Common Beginning Mistakes and Remedies

1. Pulling the rope over your head to eliminate the slack shifts your weight back and makes landings difficult. Slack can be eliminated by having the boat driven at an angled approach and by freezing the basic jumping position on the ramp and in the air.

2. Slipping on the ramp surface is caused by cutting on the ramp, by dropping a shoulder and by pulling on the handle. Keep your shoulders level and your weight evenly distributed on the skis.

3. Dropping the ski tips down in the air is caused by looking down or holding the handle away from your body. In the flight, look out, not down, and hold the handle near your waist.

Landing with your weight back results in sit down landings or falls.

Pulling the rope over your head shifts your weight back.

4. Anticipating the landing tends to move your weight back and cause a hard sit-down landing. Absorb the impact of the landing by bending your legs when your skis hit the water.

5. Getting pulled forward on the landing occurs when you have too much weight on the front of your skis or when you hold the handle away from your body. Keep your weight evenly distributed and the handle in close at your waist.

6. Skis spreading apart on the ramp is caused by having your skis apart when you make contact with the ramp or by having too much weight on the tips of your skis. Keep your weight evenly distributed on the skis and your skis close together on the approach to the ramp.

Jumping 83

BEGINNING JUMP PROGRESSION

Your first major progression after learning how to jump, is having the boat change patterns from the angled approach to the parallel approach. To achieve this, have the angle of the boat path decreased slightly after your third successful jump. Continue decreasing the angle after each successful jump until the boat is driven in a parallel path to the ramp.

After you acquire control and confidence in your jumping ability using this parallel boat path, begin to increase your boat speed and move the boat toward the 45 foot buoy. Your initial goal is to jump with control at a speed of 28 mph with the boat traveling just outside the 45 foot buoy.

The rate at which you increase your boat speed is important. It should be increased in one or two mph increments at a pace where you can maintain ski control. The best way of judging this control is by looking at your landings. If your landings are solid at a particular speed then increase the speed for the next jump. If, however, you are having difficulty landing, then keep the speed constant or lower it. When you are consistently making your landings again then increase the speed.

Moving the boat position is usually not as critical as increasing the boat speed. In fact, once the boat is traveling in a parallel path, moving the boat farther away from the ramp can help eliminate slack rope. The only real difficulty occurs when the boat has been moved too wide too soon. This problem becomes apparent if you get pulled to the right (toward the boat) when you land. If this happens have the boat remain in the same position or move it closer to the ramp until your landings are more stable.

Once the boat has been moved outside the 45 foot buoy, the boat speed increased to 28 mph and you are consistently making each jump attempt, you will be ready to start going for extra distance. The first two factors that increase distance are interrelated: spring and form.

Spring and Form

A spring is a leg extension off the top of the ramp that gives you more height and distance from the jump. Your body position before the ramp is a major determinant of how effective the spring is. You must have your left shoulder resisting the pull of the boat, skis close together, weight evenly distributed on the skis, back straight, the rope handle close at your waist and your head up, looking at the ramp.

Timing the start of the spring is critical. The impact of hitting the ramp has a tendency to force your legs down into a deeper bent knee position. You must compensate for the force of this impact by beginning your spring before you reach the bottom of the ramp.

As you feel the impact of the ramp, resist it with your legs. Then push up by straightening your legs quickly at the top of the ramp.

For an effective spring, you must establish the proper form in the air immediately after leaving the ramp. This will maximize the lift you get from the spring and allow you to glide farther in the air. After leaving the ramp, keep your back and your legs straight, your upper body pressed forward, your skis close together and your body frozen. Maintain this position until you land.

Absorb the shock of the landings with your legs. Refrain from falling back or sitting down after your skis make contact with the water. Try to land with your weight over the center of your skis and remain standing.

Photo Rick McCormick

Begin the spring before you reach the ramp, resist the impact of the ramp and then straighten your legs before leaving the top of the ramp.

Single Wake Cut

Spring and form are two means of increasing distance from the ramp. Another way is by generating additional speed by using the double wake cut.

The single wake cut is used as a temporary technique for safely teaching the double wake cut. It helps establish good spring, air and cutting form and slowly gives the beginning jumper more speed at a pace that can be handled.

The single wake cut is started from the middle of the wakes. With both hands on the handle and with the handle in near your waist cut from the wakes and aim for the center of the ramp *(see diagram)*. During this cut hold your left shoulder down and hold the handle close to your waist. Just before hitting the ramp ease your cut and establish the proper springing position.

Cutting experience will determine the proper place to initiate the single wake cut. A beginning cutter must start the cut early before the ramp to get a perspective on when to cut without taking chances. An advanced cutter must start the cut at a spot where the skis can be held on a cutting edge to the bottom of the ramp.

The single wake cut is intended as a learning aid and not a long distance jumping technique. The objective of it is to teach you to control the cut, keep your skis on a cutting edge and properly spring with added speed. Once these abilities are established move on to the double wake cut.

The single wake cut is a learning step that prepares you for the double wake cut. Advance in stages where you can control the cut.

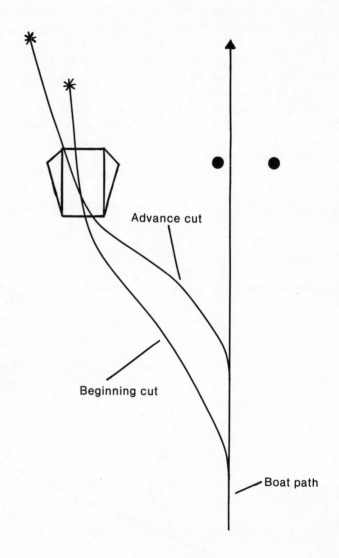

Advance cut

Beginning cut

Boat path

Single Wake Cut

DOUBLE WAKE CUT

The double wake cut generates maximum speed in the approach to the ramp. It is done in two parts: a counter cut, which positions the skier on the right side of the boat, and the cut to the ramp, which builds the extra speed for jumping long distances.

The double wake cut generates maximum speed on the approach to the ramp.

Ski Nautique

Photo Rick McCormick

Photo Rick McCormick

Counter Cut

The counter cut begins on the left side of the boat wakes and propells a skier directly beside the right side of the boat. To be effective the counter cut must get the skier to the same wide position at the same time for each jump. Getting to this position maximizes the distance to accelerate to the ramp, makes a sharp right angle turn possible and gives a jumper a good perspective on when to initiate the cut to the ramp.

Deciding when to start the counter cut largely depends on your jumping speed. The rule is the faster the boat speed the sooner the counter cut must begin. For instance, if your boat speed is 30 mph you should initiate your counter cut approximately at the 500 foot buoy. If on the other hand, your boat speed is 35 mph the counter cut should start about 50 feet before the 500 foot buoy. Your exact starting position might vary, depending on your skiing style, but generally will follow the above examples.

Counter Cut Procedure

1. Pull approximately 50 feet to the left of the boat about 200 feet before the 500 foot cut buoy (700 feet before the ramp).
2. When you are skiing at the same speed as the boat turn your skis and cut to the right. This position should be approximately 500 feet before the ramp at 30 mph and 550 feet before the ramp at 35 mph.
3. Hold this cut through both wakes, keeping your right shoulder down and the handle close to your left hip.
4. After crossing the wakes ease your pull but keep your right shoulder down and your skis on edge. Sometimes experienced jumpers increase their pulling leverage by lifting their right ski off the water.
5. Just before you reach your full width flatten your skis, remove your right hand from the handle, extend your left arm and handle straight out from your side and prepare to turn.

Keeping your right shoulder down and pulling through the wakes on the counter cut helps propel you to a position wide of the boat.

At the end of the counter cut take your skis off their cutting edges, remove your right hand from the handle and extend the handle straight out from your left side.

Cut to The Ramp

The cut to the ramp begins at the widest point of the counter cut and is held through both wakes to the bottom of the ramp. To be effective, maximum speed must be generated just before hitting the bottom of the ramp.

The force and the starting position of your cut to the ramp will vary with your cutting experience and ability. If you are a beginning cutter it should be initiated early enough to ensure that you stay in complete control and safely go over the ramp with the additional speed.

As your experience and control increase, your cutting aggressiveness should also grow. Wait later to initiate the start of your cut and begin turning your skis sharper by pulling harder at the start of the cut and pulling harder through the wakes. Your final objective is to be able to maintain a cut from the start of the turn, through the wakes, to the bottom of the ramp and still be in the proper position to spring from the ramp.

Cut to the Ramp Procedure

1. Eye your position at the end of the counter cut on either the boat and the jump or your angle in relation to the ramp.
2. To turn, grab the handle with your right hand, pull the handle in toward your chest and lead the turn with your head and shoulders.
3. During the cut keep your skis close together, your left shoulder down and the handle in at your right hip.
4. Hold the force of the cut through both wakes.
5. Ease the force of the cut after the second wake but keep your left shoulder down and your skis on a slight cutting edge until the bottom of the ramp.
6. Concentrate on obtaining the proper springing position before hitting the ramp: skis close together, weight evenly distributed, back straight, handle close to your body and your head up looking at the ramp.

Spring, Form and Landing on the Double Wake Cut

Combining the double wake cut with a good spring and good form maximizes your distance from the ramp. However, the increased amount of speed generated by the double wake cut makes the spring more difficult to achieve since you have less time to react on the ramp. For a good spring you must put more emphasis on holding your left shoulder down, initiating the spring sooner and holding the proper springing position.

A good spring will do more than give you lift off the top of the ramp. It will also place you in the proper position to maximize your glide in the air. Concentrate on holding the proper springing position before the ramp and good air form will be relatively easy to obtain.

Photo Rick McCormick

During the descent many long distance jumpers prefer to release their left hand from the handle and use their left arm for balance. Other skiers like to keep both hands on the handle to insure better control. If you are not jumping long distances (over 100 feet) there will be a tendency to have more pull on the handle during the descent. In this case, you should continue to keep both hands on the handle until you land. On the other hand, if you are a long distance jumper and landing to the side of the boat, the one handed method might feel more comfortable.

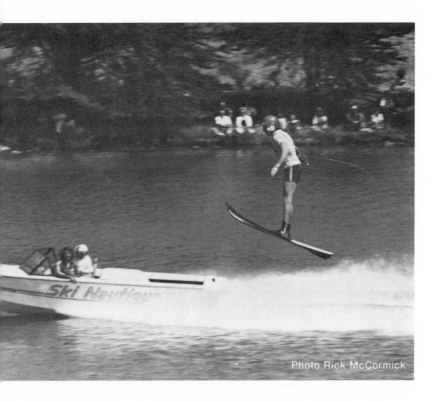

Photo Rick McCormick

6. On the ascent keep your skis close together and pointed away from the boat.
7. At the peak of the jump pull your arms in to your waist and press your body forward.
8. On the descent keep your legs straight, your body pressed forward and continue looking to the left of your landing area.
9. Land standing up with your weight evenly distributed and equally balanced on the center of your skis.
10. Absorb the shock of the landing by bending your knees and bending slightly forward at the waist.

Spring, Form and Landing Procedure
1. Keep your left shoulder down coming into the bottom of the ramp.
2. Initiate the start of the spring before reaching the bottom of the ramp.
3. Resist the impact of hitting the ramp by holding your position.
4. Complete the spring by quickly straightening your legs at the top of the ramp.
5. As you leave the top of the ramp resist the pull from the boat by keeping your left shoulder down.

Photo Rick McCormick

COMMON LONG DISTANCE JUMPING MISTAKES AND REMEDIES

Cutting

1. Drifting back before starting the cut to the ramp makes a sharp right angle turn difficult and shortens the cutting distance to the ramp. Start your cut from the widest position perpendicular to the boat.
2. Starting the cut to the ramp with slack rope pulls you forward at the start of the cut and places you in an unstable cutting position when crossing the wakes. Extend the handle straight out from your side with your left hand and pull the handle in to your chest at the start of the turn. If the problem still exists initiate your counter cut sooner.
3. Not holding the left shoulder down during the cut to the ramp reduces the speed from the cut and places you in a poor position for the spring on the ramp. Keep your left shoulder down from the start of the cut, through both wakes, to the bottom of the ramp.
4. Allowing the handle to be pulled away from your body places you in an unstable position when you hit the ramp. Keep the handle close to your body.

Spreading your skis on the ramp makes a good spring impossible to achieve.

Springing

1. Initiating the spring after hitting the ramp prevents a complete leg extension on the ramp. Start the upward springing motion before you hit the bottom of the ramp.
2. Allowing the skis to spread apart on the ramp reduces the effectiveness of the spring. On the approach to the ramp, keep your skis close together and your weight evenly distributed on both skis.
3. Throwing your body back during the spring stops the forward momentum of the spring. Push straight up from the top of the ramp and press forward in the air.
4. Bending forward at the waist on the ramp makes your body absorb the spring. Keep your back straight, the handle in at your waist and push straight up from the top of the ramp.

Photo Rick McCormick

Excessive banking is caused by lowering your right shoulder.

Form in the Air

1. Banking, allowing your skis to slide away from the pull of the boat while in the air, reduces the effectiveness of your spring and slows your momentum in the air. Keep your left shoulder down, resisting the pull from the boat, and keep the handle in close at your waist during the spring.
2. Allowing your skis to turn toward the boat places more drag on your skis and slows your air speed. Keep your skis pointed away from the boat and look to the left of the landing area.
3. Having your ski tips come up near your face slows your air speed. It is caused by having your weight too far back when leaving the top of the ramp. Push straight up from the top of the ramp and press your body forward in the air.
4. Bending forward at the waist reduces air control. It is caused by having the handle too far away from your body during the ascent. Keep the handle close to your body before the ramp, on the ramp and during the ascent.

Landings

1. Falling back on the landing is caused by having your weight too far back during the descent. Keep your weight evenly distributed and press your body forward in the air.
2. Landing with your weight on the right ski is caused by not having your shoulders level and not having your weight evenly distributed on both skis. Keep your shoulders level and your weight evenly distributed.
3. Falling forward on the landing is caused by having your weight too far forward and by not absorbing the shock of the landing with your legs and upper body. Keep your weight over the center of your skis and absorb the shock of the landings by bending your legs and bending slightly forward at the waist.

Photo Barbara Young

ADVANCED JUMP PROGRESSION

As a long distance jumper you must learn to jump safely and progress in stages where you have complete control. Push your progress within sensible limits where you have control and confidence, but never exceed your capabilities.

The most important decisions you will be making are at what boat speed to jump and when to raise the ramp height if your division requires it. You will also need to learn how to balk and when to change the position of the boat if it is necessary.

Boat Speed

Maximum allowable boat speeds range from 28 to 35 mph depending on your age and sex. To use the double wake cut at the maximum speed of your division you must first perfect your cutting and springing technique at the lower boat speeds. This will be relatively simple for those of you who have maximum boat speeds of 28 or 30 mph, since you should already be jumping at 28 mph by this stage. Those of you in the 30 mph divisions need only raise the boat speed two mph after you have learned the single wake cut.

Raising the boat speed, if your division allows 35 mph maximum, requires personal evaluation. Your boat speed should remain at 30 mph until you learn how to double wake cut with the proper spring, form and landing. After this is accomplished you should raise the speed in two mph increments, but only when you feel you will be able to handle the additional speed and maintain good form.

Falling back on the landing is caused by having your weight back during the descent.

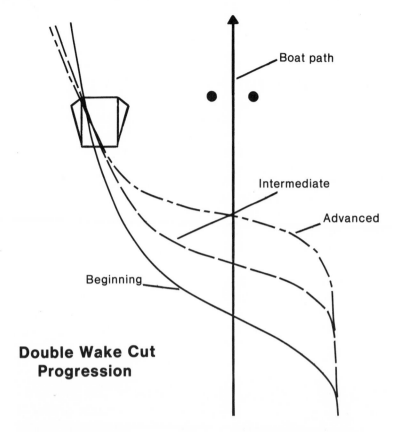

Boat path

Intermediate

Advanced

Beginning

Double Wake Cut Progression

Ramp Height

The standard ramp height is five feet and need only be raised if you are in the Men I or Men II division, at which time the ramp is raised to five and one half or six feet, depending on your level of competition. Ideally, the height of the ramp should remain at five feet until you are consistently jumping over 100 feet with good form and control. However, when you compete you have no choice but to jump the higher ramp height regardless of your skills. If you are a beginning jumper who must ski on the five and one half foot ramp, stay with the basics: single wake cut, spring and form. In the off season and the interim between tournaments change back to the lower ramp height and perfect your double wake cut, spring and form before raising the ramp height permanently.

Balk

Sometimes a cut to the ramp is initiated too late to accomplish a safe jump, or rough water makes a safe jump impossible, or maybe your body and mind just aren't ready for hitting the ramp. In these instances, knowing when and how not to go over the ramp are as important as knowing how to go over the ramp.

The balk is accomplished by letting go of the handle before reaching the bottom of the ramp and then skiing around the lower left corner without making contact. It should be initiated as soon as you decide you are not going over the ramp. The sooner the handle is released the more time you will have to safely avoid the ramp.

Balking is an integral part of sensible double wake cut jumping. Never try to take a jump when you are out of control. Release the handle and try again.

Photo Barbara Young

Boat Positioning

Proper boat positioning is also essential for long distance jumping. The boat must be driven at a distance from the ramp where you can combine the double wake cut with a spring and obtain the maximum distance from the ramp.

If you are a beginning double wake cutter you should have the boat driven just outside the 45 foot buoy. This position gives you a basis for judging your cut since you are already familiar with it. It is also an easy and consistent position to drive at.

Once you have established cutting consistency and understand your cutting capabilities, then consider moving the boat position wider. Determining if you have arrived at that stage will be dependent on your jumping skills. As a general rule, if you are not jumping at least 100 feet at 30 mph on a five foot ramp you should probably continue jumping with the boat driven next to the 45 foot buoy.

If, however, you are jumping over 100 feet and feel you can increase the speed of your cut by moving the boat position wider, then take a few practice sessions experimenting with a wider path. (The most common position is splitting the distance between the 45 and 60 foot guide buoys.) Evaluate your jumping performances at the new width and use this to base your decision on where to have the boat driven to best maximize your jumping distances.

All jumpers, beginner through long distance, should practice riding on their jump skis.

JUMP PRACTICE

Your primary goal when practicing jumping is to learn to jump long distances consistently. This is accomplished by perfecting the fundamentals described earlier: the spring, form, landing and double wake cut. The fastest way of developing these fundamentals is to structure your practice sessions according to your level of jumping.

If you are at the beginning level your main concern is learning ski control and establishing a familiarity with the ramp. This requires several jump sessions and also requires riding your jump skis as often as possible. The number of jump sessions and the duration of each will vary with your physical capabilities. Generally, most beginning jumpers will take between 10 to 15 jumps per session and anywhere from three to ten sessions a

week. Pick a schedule you feel comfortable with and does not over fatigue your body.

Once past the beginning level your object is to develop the proper spring and form. As with a beginner, this requires a large number of jump sessions. Keep in mind at this level you are learning two very important parts of jumping long distances, but you are not attempting to jump long distances. Pick an area of weakness and work on it during the entire jump session. Analyze your mistakes by looking at the basics.

As you progress further you will become more and more interested in increasing your distances in practice. At this level you should be working on the double wake cut and learning how to combine it with a good spring and good form. Using the double wake cut requires more physical effort on your part which means your body will tire quicker. Therefore, you should limit each jump session to a maximum of four to five jumps. This ensures freshness for each jump and allows you to remain strong for the entire practice.

The number of practice sessions you take a week will largely depend on the ramp height and distances you are jumping. Generally, the higher ramp heights and longer distances tire your body more and thus necessitate fewer practice sessions. In most cases, a five foot jumper can take anywhere from eight to ten sessions a week while a five and one half or six foot jumper normally takes three to five sessions a week. Use a schedule that fits your physical capabilities and allows you to be strong on each jump.

In each practice session, pick one area of weakness and dedicate the entire session to working on it. For instance, if you are having difficulty with your spring, then ease your cut and try to resolve the problem. It is difficult to try and perfect one area if all your energy and thought is going toward only jumping long distances. Concentrate on one thing at a time; you will find this method of practicing is the most beneficial.

COMPETITION

A jumper's first responsibility when going to an unfamiliar tournament site is to become familiar with the jump course. You must note the path the boat is driven, areas where you may ski close to shore or some object and areas where waves or rollers may occur in the course. Also, look at the jump and become familiar with its physical appearance; i.e. color, deck material, angle of side curtains, etc.

While waiting for your turn to jump, visualize the path you will be skiing. Picture yourself preparing for your counter cut at an approximate location and continuing through the entire jump course.

If you are able to watch other jumpers, note where they are starting their cuts and analyze the effectiveness of their decisions. For instance, if all the jumpers are drifting back before starting their cut to the ramp, perhaps the 500 foot buoy is positioned over 500 feet from the ramp or a head wind is slowing them down. Try to learn by their mistakes.

When the driver comes to pick you up for your first jump tell him the speed and boat position you desire. Make sure he understands your instructions by asking him to repeat back exactly what you have told him.

Use the first of your three tournament jumps as a warm up. If you have not skied in that jump course before, approach the first jump conservatively to become accustomed to the impact of hitting that ramp and the peculiarities of that jump course. If on the other hand, you are familiar with the jump course and you feel confident, then approach the jump like your first practice jump. In either case do not assume the driver will drive a certain way or the ramp will feel slippery or slow, be prepared for the unexpected.

Usually the most difficult adjustment when going to a tournament site is cutting. A new boat driver, different surroundings and wind conditions can make the counter cut and the cut to the ramp harder to negotiate.

Learn to use your first cut to the ramp as a guide for the two proceeding jumps and the second cut to the ramp as a guide for the last. For instance, if you are arriving at the ramp too early, perhaps your counter cut needs to be started later to force you to start your cut to the ramp later. Or if you are too late on the cut to the jump, try starting your counter cut sooner. In either case analyze your mistakes and make whatever adjustments are necessary to allow you to cut to your potential.

Difficulty adjusting to a different ramp surface can usually be attributed to a miscalculated cut: having too much speed or too little speed. These problems go away when you successfully negotiate the proper cut. However, there are instances where an extremely slow or slippery ramp can effect your spring. A slow ramp has a tendency to pitch you forward on the ramp. On slow ramps, concentrate on keeping your back straight and pulling with your left shoulder. A fast ramp tends to cause your skis to split apart and shift your weight back. When you jump on fast ramps keep your skis together on the approach and straighten your legs sooner before hitting the ramp.

The last and most important point to remember about tournament jumping is that to be successful you must try to jump like you do in practice. Avoid the temptation to exceed your limits by cutting later than you can handle or springing harder than you are accustomed to. Approach the jumps sensibly and concentrate on jumping like you do in practice.

Bob LaPoint demonstrates the proper air form used for long distance jumping.

ADVERSE WATER CONDITIONS

Jump courses are usually situated close to the shore or in a protected cove. However, ideal water and wind conditions do not always prevail and you must be prepared to jump under any circumstances. To safely maximize your jump distances you must be able to make adjustments in your counter cut, cut to the ramp and your form in the air.

There are normally three types of adverse water conditions: a head wind, a tail wind and choppy water. Each condition places more responsibility on the jumper to maintain good skiing position and to be more conscious of safety. Each condition also has a special technique to make jumping easier and safer.

A head wind slows the skier's speed. To compensate for the wind the counter cut must be started later and the pull must be held longer to reach the wide position for the cut to the ramp. The cut to the ramp does not change but the air flight becomes more critical. The tendency in a head wind is for the wind to push your ski tips up near your face. This places more drag on the skis in the air and shortens your jumping distances. During the flight keep your skis level and your body pressed forward.

Skiing with a tail wind can be an advantage since it pushes you faster on the water and pushes you farther in the air. Because of this, the counter cut must be started sooner to give you time to slow your speed before making the cut to the ramp. During the flight, the push of the wind has a tendency to cause slack rope and push the ski tips down. Both factors make landings more difficult. To eliminate these problems keep your skis pointed away from the boat and concentrate on keeping the ski tips up.

Another problem you may encounter when jumping with a tail wind is rough water at the bottom of the ramp. To overcome this obstacle, concentrate on keeping your left shoulder down, the skis on edge and holding the proper body position.

How you ski in choppy water largely depends on the degree of the chop. Small waves can be negotiated safely and effectively if you keep your skis on the cutting edge and force yourself to maintain the correct body position. Large waves, however, necessitate the realization that safe jumping is the top priority. If you elect to cut to the ramp in large chop, try to generate the majority of your speed through the wakes and keep your skis on a slight cutting edge to the bottom of the ramp. Before going over the ramp be sure you are in a solid stance, not being pulled forward or sitting back.

JUMP DRIVING

A jump driver is in a position of trust. The driving procedures used will not only determine the success of a jumper, but also the safety of a jumper.

As a driver for a beginning jumper you have two major responsibilities. First, you should help the jumper over ther ramp by compensating for skier weaknesses. And second, you must quickly get back to the jumper after a fall.

The best way of helping a beginning jumper over the ramp is by driving the proper boat pattern. The boat should be driven at a slight angle away from the ramp to keep pressure on the rope. This helps eliminate slack rope.

Another way of helping a beginning jumper is by driving boat speeds that help the skier. For instance, sometimes lowering a boat speed a few miles per hour can prevent a beginner from slipping on the ramp. Or raising the boat speed a few miles per hour can sometimes make hard sit-down landings easier. The boat driver, then, should try to adapt the boat speed to meet the skier's needs.

The other driver responsibility is to get back to the beginning jumper quickly and safely after each fall.

When a beginning jumper falls you should immediately turn the boat back to the skier and have the observer ready to offer the skier assistance.

Driving for the advanced jumper is similar to driving for a slalom skier. You must drive in a straight line, hold a constant speed, return to a skier quickly after a fall and stop the boat if there are waves or boat wakes in the jump course.

Always drive parallel to the ramp at the requested distance from the boat guide buoys. This path should be established well before the 500 foot buoy and held through the entire jump course.

Like in slalom, learn to anticipate the skier's pulls and apply the appropriate amount of throttle to keep the speed constant during the counter cut, cut to the ramp and flight in the air. Never overcompensate or apply the throttle too late. Hold the speed constant.

While driving, watch for boat waves or rollers in the jump course. If there are waves in the path of the skier or near the bottom of the ramp, stop the boat before the skier makes the cut to the ramp.

When a jumper falls, you and the observer have the responsibility of looking for the safety hand signal. If the signal has not been given or if the signal was given but appears inappropriate, then get back to the skier as quickly as possible. If the signal is given and you know the skier is OK, then make a small radius turn and come back to the skier in the same path the boat has traveled.

Whether you are driving for a beginner or an expert, you have the responsibility not to pull a fallen jumper who you feel is not in the physical or mental condition to continue jumping. Be cautious and refuse to pull a jumper if there is any question in your mind that the skier should not continue.

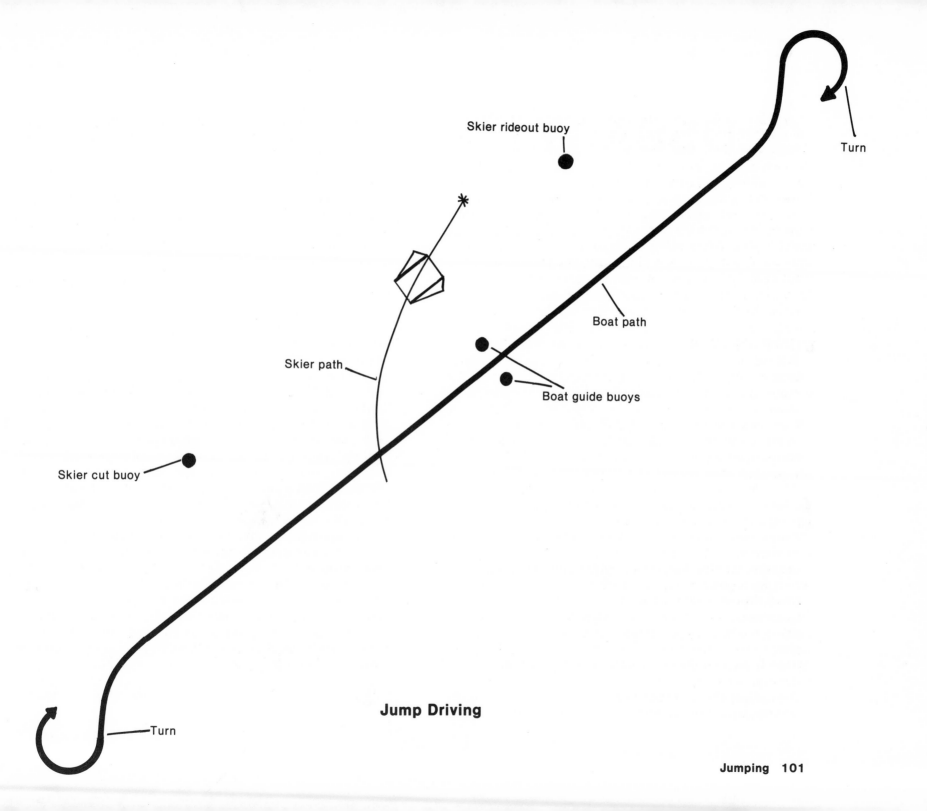

Skier rideout buoy

Boat path

Skier path

Boat guide buoys

Turn

Skier cut buoy

Turn

Jump Driving

GLOSSARY

Aprons. See side curtains.

Arm sling. An equipment device worn while jumping to hold the right arm in close at the waist.

AWSA. American Water Ski Association, P.O. Box 191, Winter Haven, FL 33880. Governing body for water ski tournaments sanctioned within the United States.

Back wash. Rolling water that results from boat wakes hitting and rebounding off stationary objects such as sea walls, piers, boats, etc.

Balk. When a jumper releases the ski rope handle and skis past or over a portion of the left side of the ramp.

Ball. See buoy.

Banking. An unstable jumping position in the air where the skis slide away from the pull of the boat and the skier is pulled toward the boat.

Bear trap. A toe hold strap that closes on the foot.

Bevel. A rounded edge of a ski. Usually refers to the bottom edge of a slalom ski.

Binding. A specially designed rubber shoe attached to the ski.

Bridle. The rope attached to the handle.

Bumps. Rolling or choppy water.

Buoys. Red and yellow plastic balls, nine inches in diameter, used to outline the slalom, trick and jump courses.

Carbon graphite. Aero space by-product used in the manufacturing of some fiberglass skis.

Chop. Waves created by wind.

Counter cut. A cut from the left side of the boat to the right side of the boat that prepares a jumper for the cut to the ramp.

Course. Buoys outlining a predetermined ski area.

Course, jump. See appendix.

Course, slalom. See appendix.

Course, trick. See appendix.

Crash. A hard fall in jumping.

Cross grip. A baseball like grip on a vertically held handle.

Cutting. Placing a ski or skis on edge and leaning away from the pull of the boat.

Divisions. Age and sex categories in competitive skiing. See appendix.

Double wake cut. A jumping cut that maximizes skier speed. It is started from the right side of the boat and held to the bottom of the ramp.

Edging. Holding a ski or skis on an edge to maintain acceleration or to initiate deceleration.

Ensolite. A rubber coated foam material used for manufacturing flotation ski vests.

EP. Exceptional performance. Rating required to ski in the National Water Ski Championships.

Expert. The fifth level of ranking in competition.

Fanny Dunk. Sitting down or falling back on a jump landing.

Fiberglass. A composite material consisting of glass fibers in resin.

Figures. Trick skiing.

Fins, boat. Stabilizing rudders on the hull of the boat.

Fins, ski. Rudders placed on the bottom rear of slalom and jump skis that aid in the maneuverability of the ski.

Flat bottom. A beginning slalom ski design.

Flattening out. Changing a ski from riding on a cutting edge to riding on the bottom surface.

Flex. The amount a ski will bend under pressure.

Foam filled. A ski construction which consists of a foam core wrapped with fiberglass.

Free style. A variation of the trick and jump events where the skier performs tricks and maneuvers, usually off the jump ramp.

Gates. Buoys that denote the starting and ending points in a course.

Glass. Fiberglass.

Green flag. In competition the green flag signifies that the boat maintained a speed in excess of the allowed tolerance in slalom.

Head wind. Skiing with the wind in your face.

Header. A forward fall.

Heel cup. A slalom ski rear heel binding.

Heel pads. Thin rubber cushions placed inside the binding and underneath the heel to prevent heel bruises.

Helicopter. A 360 degree turn executed in the air off the wake or off the jump ramp.

Hitch. See pylon.

Hit it. Audible signal used by the skier to indicate to the driver to start.

Honeycomb. A honeycomb shaped aluminum mesh used for structural strength in the inner core of some fiberglass skis.

Hook. A sharp and quick ski turn.

Jacket. An ensolite or nylon flotation vest.

Jam. See spring.

Jump ramp. See diagram.

Jump pants. Wetsuit shorts used for jumping.

Lift. Amount of height a skier gets off the top of the ramp.

Line off. A shortened slalom rope.

Master rating. The sixth highest ranking in competition.

Master board. The jump meter control board where jump distances are computed.

Meter stations. Stationary stands from which the angles of jump landings are sighted. These angles are given to the master board to compute distances from the ramp.

Nationals. National Water Ski Championships, held annually.

Observer. An extra person in the towboat used to help in skier communications and skier assistance.

Open class. The highest ranking for a tournament water skier.

Pass. A run completed in slalom, tricks or jumping.

Planing. A flat riding ski or boat.

Plate mounted binding. Bindings mounted on a plastic or metal plate.

Polypropylene. A synthetic plastic composition used for making ski ropes.

Pop. See spring.

Pull. The force from a cut.

Pylon. A ski rope towing hitch, usually positioned in the middle center of the boat.

Quick release. Specially designed safety devise used in a boat that allows the driver or observer to release the rope from the boat.

Ratings. Scales of achievement used in grading the progression of a skier's performance. The grades are: novice, third class, second class, first class, expert, master, exceptional performance, and open class.

Red flag. In competition the red flag signifies a mandatory reride.

Reinforcement straps. An additional piece of rubber placed around the heel or instep of the foot for added binding support.

Reride. In competition, when a skier re-skis a pass.

Rocker. The bow like curve in a ski.

Rollers. Rough water caused by wind or boat waves.

Sanctioned tournaments. Touraments approved by the AWSA or WWSU.

Side boards. See side curtains.

Side curtains. Sides attached to the jump ramp and positioned at an angle to prevent the jumper from skiing into the undercarriage of the ramp.

Single wake cut. A jumping cut initiated from the middle of the wakes and held to the bottom of the ramp.

Slip. Skis sliding sideways on the ramp.

Sling. A loose toehold strap that does not close tight on the foot.

Spring. Straightening the legs quickly at the top of the jump ramp.

Spray. The wall of water forced into the air during a turn of the ski.

Stepover. A trick where the skier steps over the rope with the free foot or the ski while turning 180, 360, or 540 degrees.

Tail wind. Skiing with the wind at your back.

Toehold strap. A canvas, leather or rubber strap attached to the trick bridle and used for toehold turns. See bear trap and sling.

Tow bar. See pylon.

Transition zone. The area where a skier changes from a cutting edge of the ski or skis to the bottom of the ski or skis.

Tuning. Altering the edges of a ski to change its performance.

Tunnel concave. A deep concave.

Wake. Wave created by a moving boat.

Wax. A high boiling point wax used on the surface of a jump ramp to provide a lubricant between the jump skis and the jump surface.

Worlds. World Water Ski Championships, held every other year.

Wrap around strap. Reinforcement binding strap which wraps around the foot from one side of the heel to the toe.

WWSU. World Water Ski Union. Governing body for World Water Ski Championships.

"Tricks is done, slalom is . . . ."

APPENDIX

DIVISIONS OF COMPETITION

*Open Men	13 years and over
*Open Women	13 years and over
Men I	17-24 years inclusive
Men II	25-34 years inclusive
Women	17-29 years inclusive
Senior Men	35 to 44 inclusive
Veteran Men	45 and over
Senior Women	30 years and over
Boys	13-16 years inclusive
Girls	13-16 years inclusive
Junior Boys	12 years and under
Junior Girls	12 years and under

*Must meet minimum performance standards

MAXIMUM BOAT SPEEDS

Slalom
36 mph - Open Men, Men I, Men II and Boys
34 mph - All other divisions

Jumping
35 mph - Open Men, Men I, Men II
30 mph - Open Women, Women, Sr. Women, Sr. Men, Veteran Men, Boys, Girls
28 mph - Jr. Boys and Jr. Girls

Courtesy American Water Ski Association

LINE SHORTENING SCHEDULE

1st cut — to a 18.25 meter length (59' 10½")
2nd cut — to a 16 meter length (52' 6")
3rd cut — to a 14.25 meter length (46' 9")
4th cut — to a 13 meter length (42' 7-13/16")
5th cut — to a 12 meter length (39' 4-7/16")
6th cut — to an 11.25 meter length (36' 10-7/8")

Slalom Times — .1 Second

		Allowed Times	
MPH	Actual	(±1 mph)	(±½ mph)
22	26.3	25.2-27.5	25.7-26.9
24	24.1	23.2-25.1	23.7-24.6
26	22.3	21.5-23.1	21.9-22.7
28	20.7	20.0-21.4	20.4-21.0
30	19.3	18.7-19.9	19.0-19.6
32	18.1	17.6-18.6	17.9-18.3
34	17.0	16.5-17.5	16.8-17.2
36	16.1	15.7-16.5	15.9-16.3

Jump Times — .1 Second

22	8.8	8.4-9.3	8.6-9.0
24	8.1	7.8-8.4	7.9-8.3
26	7.5	7.2-7.8	7.3-7.6
28	6.9	6.7-7.2	6.7-7.1
30	6.5	6.3-6.7	6.3-6.7
32	6.1	5.9-6.3	6.0-6.2
33	5.9	5.7-6.1	5.8-6.0
34	5.7	5.6-5.9	5.6-5.8
35	5.6	5.4-5.7	5.5-5.6

OFFICIAL SLALOM COURSE

Not to Scale

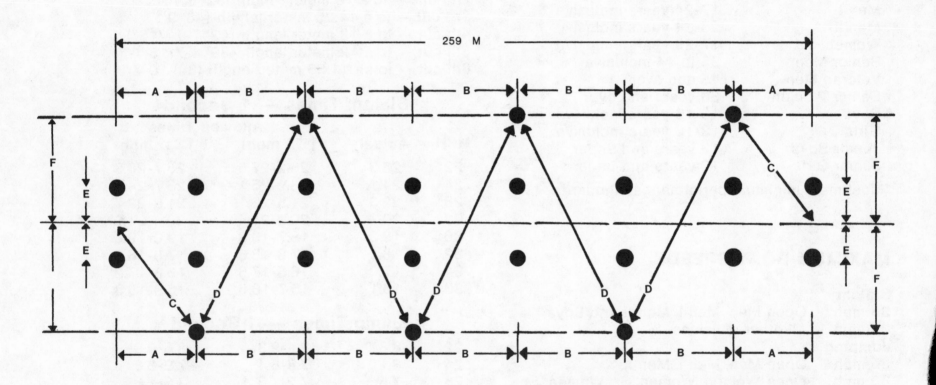

DIMENSIONS:

	259M	=	849'8.8"
A =	27M	=	88'7.0"
B =	41M	=	134'6.1"
C =	29.347M	=	96'3.4"
D =	47.011M	=	154'2.8"
E =	1.25M	=	4'1.2"
F =	11.5M	=	37'8.8"

ALLOWED RANGES ON DIMENSIONS:

259M OVERALL: 257.705-260.295M=845'5.9"-853'11.8"
A (27M)   26.730- 27.270M= 87'8.4"- 89'5.6"
B (41M)   40.590- 41.410M=133'2.0"-135'10.3"
C (29.347M)   29.054- 29.640M= 95'3.9"- 97'2.9"
D (47.011M)   46.541- 47.481M=152'8.3"-155'9.3"
E (1.25M)   1.125- 1.375M= 3'8.3"- 4'6.1"
F (11.5M)   11.385- 11.615M= 37'4.2"- 38'1.3"

Courtesy American Water Ski Association

TRICK POINT VALUES

DESCRIPTION	WATER TURNS				WAKE TURNS			
	TRICK NO.	CODE	2 SKIS	1 SKI	TRICK NO.	CODE	2 SKIS	1 SKI
180° FB	1	B	30*	60*	15	WB	50*	80*
180° BF	2	F	30*	60*	16	WF	50*	80*
360° FF	3	O	40*	90*	17	WO	110*	150*
360° BB		OB	40*	90*	18	WBB	160*	210*
540° FB		5B	50	110	19	W5B	240*	310*
540° BF		5F	50	110	20	W5F	250*	320*
720° FF		7F	60	130	21	W7F	400*	400*
720° BB		7B	60	130	22	W7B	430*	430*
900° FB					23	W9B	550	550
900° BF						W9F	550	550
Stepover 180° FB	4	LB	80*	120	24	WLB	110*	180
Stepover 180° BF	5	LF	70*	110	25	WLF	110*	160
Stepover 360° FF					26	WLO	200*	260*
Stepover 360° BB					27	WLBB	200*	260*
Stepover 540° FB					28	WL5B	300*	420*
Stepover 720° FF						WL7F		480*
Double Stepover 540° FB						WL5LB		500*
Stepover 540° BF					29	WL5F	300*	420*
Stepover 720° BB						WL7B		500*
Double Stepover 540° BF						WL5LF		500*
Toehold 180° FB	6	TB		100*	30	TWB		150*
Toehold 180° BF	7	TF		120*	31	TWF		180*
Toehold 360° FF	8	TO		220*	32	TWO		300*
Toehold 360° BB	9	TBB		250*	33	TWBB		330*
Toehold 540° FB	10	T5B		350*	34	TW5B		500
Toehold 720° FF		T7F		450				
Toehold 540° BF	11	T5F		350*	35	TW5F		500
Toehold S'over 180° FB					36	TWLB		320
Toehold S'over 180° BF					37	TWLF		380
Toehold S'over 360° FF					38	TWLO		450*
Sideslide	12	S	20*	70*				
Toehold Sideslide	13	TS		150				
Wrapped T'hold Sideslide	14	WTS		230				
Somersault Forward					39	WflipF	500	500
Somersault Backward					40	WflipB	450	450

*Denotes tricks with allowable reverses. Reverses are the same value as the basic trick.

Courtesy American Water Ski Association

HAND SAFETY SIGNALS

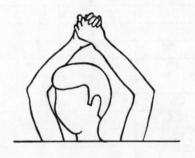

Faster   **Turn Around**   **Speed OK**   **Same Speed**

Slower   **Back to the Dock**   **I'm OK**   **Stop**